Legislation and the Courts

Edited by
MICHAEL FREEMAN

Dartmouth

Aldershot • Brookfield USA • Singapore • Sydney

Published by
Dartmouth Publishing Company Limited
Gower House
Croft Road
Aldershot
Hants GU11 3HR
England

Dartmouth Publishing Company
Old Post Road
Brookfield
Vermont 05036
USA

Coventry University

British Library Cataloguing in Publication Data
Legislation and the courts. – (Issues in law and society)
   1. Statutes – Great Britain   2. Legislation – Great Britain
   I. Freeman, M. D. A. (Michael David Alan), 1943–
   344.1'0822

Library of Congress Cataloging-in-Publication Data
Legislation and the courts / edited by Michael Freeman.
        p.   cm. — (Issues in law and society series)
     Includes bibliographical references.
     ISBN 1–85521–846–1 (hbk.). — ISBN 1–85521–853–4 (pbk.)
      1. Law—Great Britain—Interpretation and construction.
  2. Judicial process—Great Britain.   I. Freeman. Michael D. A.
  II. Series.
  KD691.L44   1997
  348.42'02—dc21   96–39522
                                         CIP

ISBN 1 85521 846 1 (HB)
ISBN 1 85521 853 4 (PB)

Printed and bound in Great Britain by
Biddles Limited, Guildford and King's Lynn

PO2164.
23-9-96

Contents

List of Contributors

Michael Freeman is Professor of English Law, University College London.

The Rt. Hon. Lord Renton QC is the former Chairman of the Committee on the Preparation of Legislation and the President of the Statute Law Society. He was a Member of Parliament from 1945 to 1979 and held ministerial posts in Fuel and Power and the Home Office.

Roger Rideout is Professor of Labour Law, University College London.

Jacqueline Dyson is Senior Lecturer in Laws, University College London.

Margot Horspool is Senior Lecturer in Laws and Deputy Director of the Centre for the Law of the European Union, University College London.

Richard Gardiner is Lecturer in Laws, University College London.

Stephen Guest is Reader in Legal Theory, University College London.

1   The Modern English Approach to Statutory Construction

Michael Freeman

It is surprising how little attention has been given to the process of statutory construction. Whether this is in spite of or because of our emphasis on parliamentary supremacy is an open question. Our attachment for so long to formalistic reasoning may be at least as important an explanation.

But, whatever, the perception of legislation as a 'stitch in time' rather than the true fabric of the law long held sway in a country dominated by the pragmatism, the induction of the common law. It was Lord Scarman, then chairman of the new Law Commission, who, in 1968, observed this with his usual elegance in *Law Reform – The New Pattern*.[1] In 1974, when he gave his *Hamlyn* lectures *English Law – The New Dimension*, he was still able to refer, accurately I believe, to

> The modern English judge [who] ... sees enacted law as an exception to, a graft upon, or a correction of, the customary law in his hands: he gives unswerving loyalty to the enacted word of Parliament, but he construes that word strictly, in its statutory context, and always upon the premise, usually unspoken, that Parliament legislates against the background of an all-embracing customary law.[2]

It was consonant with this view that Lord Simonds could refer to the filling in of gaps in a statute – Lord Denning having advocated this[3] – as 'a naked usurpation of the legislative function under the thin disguise of interpretation.'[4]

But, of course, today the construction of statutes is one of the most important of judicial functions. Because the common law itself represents the basic fabric of the law, the practice is that statutes are drafted in the fullest detail and the assumption is that it deals only with those cases which fall within its actual wording. Continental theory, by contrast, treats statutes as the basis of the law: these tend to be drafted in a very general and abstract way, the task being left to the courts to fill in the details of the statutory provisions by reference to a presumed legislative intention. Further, it is generally accepted that gaps in a statute may be filled by analogical reasoning on the basis that the legislature might be presumed to have desired to cover such cases if it had had these in contemplation.

It would seem, therefore, that the English approach is primarily based on ascertaining the plain meaning of the words used,[5] whereas that of the civil law is directed to ascertaining the intention of the legislature.[6] The belated acceptance that English courts may have recourse to *travaux préparatoires*[7] may reflect something of a shift, but too much should not be read into relaxation.

It is traditional to refer to three 'rules' of statutory construction, though they are better described as 'canons' or 'conventions'.[8] That there are thought to be three such 'rules' can only be explained historically. The earliest 'rule' was formulated in *Heydon's case* in 1584.[9] The 'mischief rule', as it came to be known, was repeated by Sir Edward Coke, and was dominant in the practice of the courts until the nineteenth century. The growth of parliamentary supremacy and the articulation of the separation of powers doctrine led, simultaneously with the emergence of the 'will theories' of law,[10] to the development in the early part of the nineteenth century of, what became known as, the literal rule. Thus, in 1827, Lord Chief Justice Tenderden could refer to the dangers of giving effect to the equity of a statute: it was better and safer, he thought, to rely on and abide by the plain words of the statute.[11]

The move to literalism was tempered by the development of the golden rule.[12] At times since then the literal rule has seemed to be very much in the ascendant. And yet there is considerable force in the remark of Lord Diplock in 1975 that 'if one looks back to the actual decisions of this House [that is: the House of Lords] on questions of statutory construction over the last thirty years, one cannot fail to be struck by the evidence of a trend away from the purely literal towards the purposive construction of statutory provisions.'[13]

It is wrong to give the impression that there are now three distinct 'rules' of statutory construction.[14] They have become fused. Driedger put it thus: 'First it was the spirit and not the letter, then the letter and not the spirit, and now the spirit and the letter'.[15] There seems now to be just one 'rule' of interpretation, a revamped version of the literal rule which requires the general context[16] and purpose to be taken into consideration before any decision is reached concerning the ordinary (or, where appropriate, the technical[17]) meaning of statutory words. The golden rule is a qualification of this, so that if the judge considers the application to the words in their ordinary sense would produce an absurd result which cannot reasonably be supposed to be the intention of the legislature, he may apply them in any secondary meaning they are capable of bearing.

The search for legislative intent, however illusory this may be,[18] has led the courts to develop also a number of conventions as a means of searching out intent. These may be classified as grammatical rules, such as the *ejusdem generis* rule, or the rule *expressio unius exclusio alterius*, and various presumptions, such as those restricting the construction of statutes which interfere with existing rights affecting the liberty of the subject, or which are penal in effect. But, although the reports are full of instances where such rules have been ostensibly applied, they are very apt to dissolve away like chaff before the wind wherever the court feels at all strongly that another interpretation is to be preferred.[19] In such cases the court may invoke the so-called 'rule in *Heydon's* case',[20] the mischief rule, or in more modern terminology the 'purposive rule', which forms a platform for a broader approach.

As for the notion that the court has no power to fill 'gaps' in legislation, very respectable authority will be found in favour of this, yet if one looks at the way courts actually construe statutes, it becomes apparent that they are frequently engaged in doing just this very thing. Indeed, there are many statutes which would prove barely workable if there were not some judicial freedom in this respect.[21]

More than a century ago the great common law scholar, Sir Frederick Pollock, wrote of what he perceived to be the approach of the judiciary: 'Parliament generally changes the law for the worse ... the business of judges is to keep the mischief of its interference within the narrowest possible bounds'.[22] But compare this with Lord Mustill, speaking for all members of the House of Lords, in 1994:

> I must own up to reservations about the reliability of generalised presumptions and maxims when engaged in the task of finding out what Parliament intended by a particular form of words, for they too readily confine the court to a perspective which treats all statutes, and all situations to which they apply, as if they were the same. This is misleading, for the basis of the rule is no more than simple fairness, which ought to be the basis of every legal rule.[23]

In this case statute had created a new procedural power enabling an arbitrator to dismiss a claim for inordinate and inexcusable delay in pursuing it. The statute did not contain a provision making it clear whether it was to be retrospective or not. The case arose before the statute came into force. The claimants in an arbitration contended that the presumption against retrospectivity required a restrictive interpretation of the statute: the respondents sought an order dismissing the claim. The House of Lords held the statute was retrospective. The presumption was investigated. The conclusion, that at root it rested on fairness, led the highest court to countenance retrospectivity in the particular context (delay in pursuing a claim), where it is clear that it would not have come to the same conclusion had it, for example, led to the characterization as criminal of past conduct which was lawful when it took place, or in the alterations to the antecedent natural, civil or familial status of individuals.

Attitudes have undoubtedly changed. In many ways the House of Lords' decision in *Pepper v Hart* symbolized this change.[24] The House of Lords held that, having regard to the purposive approach to construction of legislation the courts had adopted in order to give true effect to the intention of the legislation, the rule prohibiting courts from referring to parliamentary material as an aid to statutory construction should be relaxed so as to permit reference to parliamentary materials where the legislation was ambiguous or obscure or the literal meaning led to an absurdity, the material relied on consisted of statements by a minister or other promoter or the Bill which led to the enactment of the legislation, together with such other parliamentary material as was necessary to understand such statements and their effect and the statements relied upon were clear. Yet within three years[25] the House of Lords was echoing warnings issued long before the rule was relaxed. Lord Reid, in 1968, gave as a justification for the non-admissibility of parliamentary debates 'purely practical reasons' namely 'it would add greatly to the time and expense involved in preparing cases … if Counsel were expected to read all the debates in Hansard, and it would often be impracticable for Counsel to get access to at least the older reports of debates in select committees of the House of Commons; moreover, in a very large proportion of cases such a search, even if practicable, could throw no light on the question before the court'.[26] In 1995, with *Pepper v Hart* entrenched and the rule relaxed, Lord Browne-Wilkinson, who gave the main speech in *Pepper v Hart*, was compelled to refer to, what he considered, 'an improper use of the relaxed rule introduced by *Pepper v Hart* which, if properly used, can be a valuable aid to construction when Parliament has directly considered the point in issue and passed the legislation on the basis of the ministerial statement.' But 'it provides no assistance to a court and is capable of giving rise to much expense and delay if attempts are made to widen the category of materials that can be looked at … Judges should be astute to check such misuse of the new rule by making appropriate orders as to costs wasted.'[27] But, was it not inevitable that once the rule was relaxed, there would be attempts to relax it further? This is the way of the common law, and we should not expect differences when it comes to statutory construction.

And relaxations have taken place.[28] There is no doubt that courts have admitted extrinsic materials to interpret legislation which is neither ambiguous nor obscure. Nor is it surprising that the courts, following earlier precedents relating to treaties and European legislation should have held that, where a court is seeking to construe a statute purposively and consistently with any relevant European legislation, or the object of the legislation under consideration is to introduce into English law the provisions of an international convention or European directive, the court may adopt a more flexible approach to the admissibility of parliamentary materials than that established for the construction of a particular provision of purely domestic legislation, such as the tax legislation which was in issue in both *Pepper v Hart* and *Melluish v BMI (No 3) Ltd*.[29]

Whether the change effected by the House of Lords in *Pepper v Hart* should be considered 'a good thing' depends on what one considers the role of the judiciary to be. Because theory has penetrated all too little into accounts of statutory construction, this has hardly been explored, at least in England. If, as I argue elsewhere,[30] the judges can be a power for good – as shown, I believe, in the activist approach to judicial review – by redressing imbalances caused by failures of the political process, by rescuing legislation from the dead hand of history, then the assumption that *Pepper v Hart* is necessarily a force for good may be challenged. If we are to see legislation as a living organism, rather than a historical product, do we want our judges in constructing it to be forever looking backwards to commission reports, ministerial statements and so on? The relaxation in the rule about *travaux préparatoires* privileges the historical over the contemporary.

This collection of essays examines contemporary approaches to statutory construction in England, both in the context of three very different areas of law (labour law, tax law and child law) and more broadly within the wider world. It is hoped that it throws light on the state of statutory construction in England today.

Notes

1 See Sir Leslie Scarman, *Law Reform – The New Pattern* (London: RKP, 1968), p. 46.
2 Sir Leslie Scarman, *English Law – The New Dimension* (London: Stevens, 1974), p. 3.
3 In *Seaford Court Estates Ltd v Asher* [1949] 2 K.B. 481, 498–99.
4 In *Magor and St Mellons R.D.C. v Newport Corporation* [1952] A.C. 189, 191.
5 A good statement of this is in Lord Simon's judgment in *Maunsell v Olins* [1975] A.C. 373, 391.
6 On which see John H. Merryman, *The Civil Law Tradition* (Stanford, Ca: Stanford University Press, 1969), chs. IV–VIII.
7 In *Pepper (Inspector of Taxes) v Hart* [1993] A.C. 593.

 8   Holmes J. referred to them as 'axioms of experience' (*Boston Sand v U.S.* 108 U.S. 37).
 9   (1584) 3 Co. Rep. 7 b.
10   Associated principally with Jeremy Bentham and John Austin.
11   *Brandling v Barrington* [1827] 6 B and C 467, 475.
12   Often attributed to Baron Parke in *Becke v Smith* (1836) 2 M and W 191, 195, but it can be traced back earlier, for example to Parker C.B. in *Mitchell v Torrup* (1766) Park. 227.
13   In *Carter v Bradbeer* [1975] 2 All E.R. 158, 161.
14   As recently as 1973 Lord Simon in *Cheng v Governor of Pentonville Prison* [1973] A.C. 931 said 'English law was not able to establish "authoritatively" any "hierarchy" between the three.'
15   *The Construction of Statutes* (Toronto: Butterworths, 1974), p. 2.
16   See, for example, *Davis v Johnson* [1978] 1 All E.R. 1132.
17   See *Farrell v Alexander* [1977] A.C. 59.
18   See Gerald C. McCallum in R. Summers (ed.), *Essays in Legal Philosophy* (Oxford: Basil Blackwell, 1968), p. 237.
19   See the well-known case of *Liversidge v Anderson* [1942] A.C. 206.
20   As in *Applin v Race Relations Board* [1974] 2 All E.R. 73.
21   See to this effect Lord Reid in *Federal Steam Navigation v D.T.I.* [1974] 2 All E.R. 97, 100.
22   *Essays on Jurisprudence and Ethics* (London: Macmillan, 1882), p. 85.
23   *L'Office Cherifien des Phosphates v Yamashita-Shinnion Steamship Co. Ltd.* [1994] 2 WLR 39, 48.
24   *Op. cit.*, note 7.
25   In *Melluish v BMI (No. 3) Ltd* [1995] 4 All E.R. 453.
26   In *Beswick v Beswick* [1968 A.C. 58, 73–74, followed by Viscount Dilhorne in *Davis v Johnson* [1978] 1 All E.R. 1132, 1147.
27   *Op. cit.*, note 25, at p. 468.
28   See *Warwickshire C.C. v Johnson* [1993] 1 All E.R. 299, *Stubbings v Webb* [1993] 2 WLR 120 and *Chief Adjudications Officer* [1993] 2 WLR 292 (where Hansard was used to confirm an interpretation reached without it).
29   See *Three Rivers D.C. v Bank of England (No. 2)* [1996] 2 All E.R. 363 *per* Clarke J.
30   See my 'Positivism and Statutory Construction: An Essay in the Retrieval of Democracy' in S. Guest (ed.), *Positivism Today* (Aldershot: Dartmouth, 1996).

2 The Evolution of Modern Statute Law and its Future

The Rt. Hon. Lord Renton QC

I propose to examine how our statute law has evolved, to what problems it gives rise and what should be done about them. I shall not deal with secondary legislation, such as royal proclamations, orders in council or statutory instruments, voluminous and far-reaching though they are and always have been. I shall confine myself to statute law, not its substance, but its enactment, form and drafting, and its application.

No civilized society can survive without the rule of law, and no democracy is worthy of the name unless the representatives of the people have the last word in deciding what the statute law should be and how it is drafted, made known and enforced. It took seven centuries to achieve this.

Some Historical Insights

Parliament started in the late thirteenth century, but Queen Anne in 1707 was the last monarch to refuse to give an Act royal assent. Since then Parliament has had the last word. Even so, to this day, every Act of Parliament still starts by saying, 'Be it enacted by the Queen's most Excellent Majesty, by and with the advice and consent of the Lords Spiritual and Temporal, and Commons in this Parliament assembled, and by the authority of the same'. This is a charming tribute to the monarch, which our Queen so well deserves – although she cannot stop us! However, it was not until the Parliament Act of 1911 that the democratically elected House of Commons was able to outvote and overrule the House of Lords but it can only do this after a delay of one session. The original two sessions were reduced to one session by the Parliament Act of 1949. Of course on Finance Bills the Lords have no power to overrule or delay the Commons.

We still regard Magna Carta as our oldest statute. It started as an ultimatum by the clergy and barons to King John in 1215 but became a statute when ratified by Simon de Montfort's Parliament in 1265 and again by the Model Parliament in 1295. Only four of its chapters remain. The rest have been repealed and replaced. The late Lord Gardiner got into real trouble when he tried to have the rest of it repealed!

Magna Carta was in Latin and so were all statutes until Edward I came to the throne in 1272, when Norman French was often used as well, until Henry Tudor, a Welshman, became king in 1485. He robustly insisted that only English should be used. Even so, Norman French is still used for informing Parliament of the royal assent: 'La Reine le veult', says the Clerk of the Crown.

Apart from Magna Carta, the earliest statute still partly in force is Chapter I of the Statute of Marlborough of 1267 dealing with distraint of chattels. The most important medieval statute partly in force is the Justice of the Peace Act, 1361, which in a dozen lines requires the appointment of magistrates and gives them the wide powers they still have.

Under the Tudors, although most legislation continued to be introduced by the king's ministers, each House of Parliament became free to amend it and even to initiate legislation. Of course, Henry VIII decided to amend statutes himself and ministers increasingly in the past 30 years have tried to copy him! More about this later.

By the time Edward VI came to the throne in 1547, statutes had become so numerous and so obscurely drafted that the highly intelligent royal teenager must have echoed public opinion when he said, 'I would wish that ... the superfluous and tedious statutes were bought into one sum together and made plain and short to the intent that men might better understand them'. In other words he mainly wanted consolidation, and so later did James I and Francis Bacon but there was no serious attempt to repeal obsolete statutes until the mid-nineteenth century and, although in the late nineteenth century there were some major pieces of consolidation, there was no systematic and regular consolidation until the Act of 1949.

In the seventeenth century, Parliament was mainly concerned with constitutional and religious conflicts of matters of principle. Oliver Cromwell, whose first constituency I had and the Prime Minister now has, was not much interested in legislation, although as a backbencher he tried to prevent parts of the Fens from being drained. When he became Lord Protector, however, he dissolved Parliament and governed largely by detailed and restrictive proclamations and decreed that the Fens should be drained!

By contrast, legislation which followed the Restoration in 1660 dealt well with matters of principle: the Clarendon Code, the Statute of Frauds, the Habeas Corpus Act, and later the Bill of Rights, the Act of Settlement and the Act of Union with Scotland in 1706: all of these contained well-drafted statements of principle which have stood the test of time.

In the rest of the eighteenth century, however, and well into the nineteenth, there was much legislation which was too detailed and incomprehensible. The drafting varied. There was no consistent style or method. It was done mainly by lawyers in each department of state, especially in what became the Home Office, which was and is responsible for everything not allocated to any other department.

An astonishing thing about our legislation was that from earliest times until 1796 it was not regularly promulgated to the people, in spite of the rule that ignorance of the law is no defence. Statutes were sent to the Sheriffs each session but, until printing started in 1484, few people saw them. The judges were kept informed about them and, as there was no parliamentary system for repeal and consolidation, it was for the judges to decide which laws had become obsolete and could be disregarded. Sometimes judges ignored statutes altogether, or declared them to be void because they were 'against common right and reason ... or impossible to be performed'. I daresay some judges these days feel tempted to declare some of our statutes void for various reasons! In 1796 Parliament at last required that its legislation be promulgated throughout the land.

After the great Reform Act of 1832 dissatisfaction grew and several Statute Law Commissions were appointed. The first, in 1835, criticized 'the imperfections in the statute law' but nothing was done about it until the Statute Law Revision Acts were started in 1861. The Act of 1867 repealed 300 statutes. It was not until 1887 that it even became the regular practice to publish the annual volume of statutes.

Drafting

As to drafting: in 1869 the Parliamentary Counsel Office was started, by the Treasury. The Home Officer lawyer, Henry Thring, who later became a peer, was appointed with only one assistant. They drafted most government legislation but practising barristers later drafted some statutes. Thus Chalmers drafted the Sale of Goods Act 1893, and Chitty and Underhill the Law of Property Acts in the early 1920s. Not until 1917 was a third Parliamentary Counsel appointed, and a fourth in 1930. Now there are 33 in Whitehall and 9 in Edinburgh.

In 1875 the House of Commons appointed a Select Committee to consider 'Whether any and what means can be adopted to improve the manner and language of current legislation'. They thought things were improving with the appointment of the then small Parliamentary Counsel Office but criticized the habit of legislation by reference. They recommended that there should be explanatory memoranda, that model clauses might be prescribed for general use, and that there should be an Interpretation Act, which was enacted in 1889. Explanatory memoranda were eventually attached to Bills when first introduced to each House but not at later stages. Legislation by reference continued unabated.

Since 1946 the quantity of legislation has grown: the number of statutes each session, and the length and detailed complexity of most of them have increased. In one full volume with 1 230 pages of modest size are contained the statutes of 1946 but the statutes for 1993 are in three volumes with 2 667 much bigger pages, plus the table of contents of 66 pages.

In 1965 the two Law Commissions were started, to propose law reforms and 'keep under review all the law with a view to its systematic development, including in particular codification, elimination of anomalies, repeals, reduction of the number of separate enactments – and the simplification and modernisation of the law'. They have many achievements to their credit but it has been impossible for them to keep up with the ever-increasing amount of government legislation. In recent years, with Mr Justice Brooke as chairman, the Commission has made real efforts to simplify drafting.

The Renton Committee

In November 1971 a House of Commons Select Committee on Procedure recommended that the Government should appoint a committee to review the form, drafting, amendment and preparation of legislation, and in May 1973 the Committee on the Preparation of Legislation was appointed with fourteen members, of whom I had the honour to be made chairman. It was the first inquiry of its kind for a hundred years. The other members had a variety of valuable expertise and experience and included a former First Parliamentary Counsel in Whitehall and a former Chief Parliamentary Draftsman in Scotland. The then Chairman of the Law Commission for England and Wales was a member and so was a Scottish duke who was an early expert on the use of computers.

Our terms of reference were: 'With a view to achieving greater simplicity and clarity in statute law, to review the form in which public bills are drafted'.

We heard evidence from the most senior judges on both sides of the Border, each of whom complained of the detailed complexity of statutes and said that the intention of Parliament should be made clear by stating the purpose of each statute or part of a statute, even when some detailed provisions are necessary, as in Finance Acts or when the rights and duties of people have to be spelt out.

After two years hard labour, we put forward 81 recommendations, most of which involved making changes but only 40 of them have been wholly or mainly implemented.

Our most important proposals included recommendation 13 which says, 'The use of statement of principle should be encouraged; where detailed guidance is called for, in addition, it should be given in schedules'. And even more important is no. 15 which says, 'Statements of Purpose should be used when they are the most convenient method of clarifying the scope and effect of legislation; when so used they should be contained in clauses and not in preambles'. We added in recommendation 74: 'Detailed financial provisions should be made easier to understand by broad statements of intention'.

These recommendations were inspired by the evidence the senior judges gave us. They have been largely ignored, although the present Lord Chancellor has sometimes introduced useful purpose clauses, for example, in the Children Act 1989, the Courts and Legal Services Act 1990.

Statement of Purpose

Our ever-increasing volume of legislation contains a vast amount of detail, much of which cannot be avoided when people's rights and duties *vis-à-vis* the state are defined as in legislation concerning the activities of statutory bodies, local authorities and companies. But such detailed provisions are generally better understood when accompanied by statements of purpose to make clear the intention of Parliament. Also, that would sometimes make it less necessary to include some of the details.

There is also a large amount of detail which is intended to cover hypothetical cases, which civil servants instructing the draftsman insist should be covered. Also MPs often ask ministers piloting Bills what would happen in hypothetical circumstances which they describe, sometimes because constituents want to know. When dealing with such matters 30 years ago I used to reply, 'The principle is clearly stated and it will be for the Courts to decide whether your constituent's case comes within it or not'. In those days one 'got away with it', but ministers now feel compelled to cover such hypothetical cases by amending the Bill at its next stage; and there is still a great reluctance to use statements of purpose. Peers too occasionally are hypothetically curious. The trouble about trying to cover every imaginable situation is that in practice we fail to anticipate some of those cases which actually occur and come before the courts. So it really is essential for us to move from the particular to the general, from detail to principle. The great Sir Edward Coke said 400 years ago, 'The lawmakers could not possibly set down all cases in express terms'. But we go on trying to do it.

Our Committee also dealt with legislation by reference and recommended that previous statutes should be amended by the textual method as generously as possible. This has been done, and the preparation of Statutes in Force, Halsbury's Statutes and Consolidation Acts has become easier as a result.

Of course, we consider in depth the eternal conflict between the public demand for clear and simple language and the need to achieve certainty of legal effect. We decided that the draftsman should not be required to sacrifice legal certainty for simplicity of language. Those who draft our statutes have an exceedingly arduous and difficult task. They are highly skilled and well-trained people who are obliged to follow the instructions given by departmental civil servants. They have to work under tremendous pressure of time. When things go wrong and obscurity or ambiguity results, the draftsmen are generally 'more sinned against that sinning', and are mostly not to blame. But they do seem a bit obstinate sometimes in resisting good suggestions for improvement.

It is often possible to achieve legal certainty in simple language, and they do so increasingly in Australia, Canada and New Zealand, countries where the Renton Report has received a much more favourable reception that it has in Whitehall.

I am not being entirely frivolous when I remind you that Moses was an excellent draftsman. When he said, 'Thou shall not steal', everyone knew what he meant. But we have the Theft Act 1978, with 36 sections, which have given rise to many problems of interpretation, which have had to be considered many times by the Court of Appeal and the House of Lords.

The Hansard Society Report

Since our Committee reported in 1975 our own legislation has increased enormously in volume, in detail and in complexity. So much so that even specialist professional advisers are sometimes perplexed by it: accountants in particular are worried by Finance Acts. The Hansard Society in 1991 decided to hold its own inquiry with Lord Rippon of Hexham, one of the Statute Law Society's Vice-Presidents, as Chairman, assisted by 18 other distinguished people. They dealt at length with subordinate legislation as well as with statutes. Their many recommendations included some which went further than some of ours.

Their recommendation 35 was especially valuable: 'Some means should be found of informing the citizen, his lawyers and the courts of the intention underlying the words of a statute'. Of course, my own view is that this would be best done by statements of purpose in the statute itself but they said it should be done by publishing notes, explaining the purpose and intended effect of each section and schedule. These notes would be laid before Parliament but would not require parliamentary approval.

With deepest respect, may I say that I would rather have the intention of Parliament clearly declared in the statute, instead of having to be explained afterwards.

However, I do strongly agree with their recommendations that the Parliamentary Counsel Office and its policy should be the responsibility of the Attorney-General instead of the Prime Minister. In Scotland the Parliamentary Draftsmen are the responsibility of the Lord Advocate, who is now always in the Lords, as recommended by our Committee. Scottish legislation (dare I say it?) is sometimes better drafted! Prime Ministers are much too busy with great affairs of state to argue much with the officials who advise them on these matters, or to deal with drafting and massive legal problems. Prime ministerial responsibility should pass to the Attorney-General. In theory each minister is responsible for the drafting of the Bills he introduced but in practice no minister has time to master the mass of detail which lengthy Bills contain.

Scrutiny of Delegated Legislation

In the House of Lords last year we appointed a Delegated Powers Scrutiny Committee: 'To report whether the provisions of any bill inappropriately delegate legislative power, or whether they subject the exercise of legislative power to an inappropriate degree of Parliamentary Scrutiny'. We were worried about Henry VIII clauses, which gave ministers powers to amend statutes by subordinate legislation. I am glad to say that Lord Rippon became the first chairman of this Committee and that Lord Alexander of Weedon is now doing it. Their reports are proving extremely valuable in our scrutiny of Government legislation.

Judicial Interpretation of Statutes

I do not know to what extent judicial interpretation influences drafting but drafting greatly influences judicial interpretation of statutes. From earliest times judges have found it difficult to interpret them, and most of the time of appellate judges is now taken up in doing so. Parliament has never required the judges to do so in any particular way. The Interpretation Act merely provides some definitions and minor assumptions. So the judges have made their own well-known rules of interpretation.

The first was the Mischief Rule in 1584: to find out the intention of Parliament it was necessary to discover the mischief for which the common law did not provide and what was the remedy Parliament chose to cure it. That rule still applies when relevant. Later came the Golden Rule, which said that, if the whole statute leads to inconsistency, absurdity or inconvenience, the court should give it another meaning that makes more sense. This caused problems and led to the Literal Rule: if the words of the statute which apply to the case being tried are clear, they must be followed, however unjust the result. Then came 'the Diplock principle', that the court must give effect to what the words would mean to those whose conduct the statute regulates.

In the past 50 years the judges have gradually adopted the 'purposive rule', and under it they try to discover what Parliament intended, but this was subject to the exclusionary rule, which forbade judges from considering *travaux préparatoires*, including White Papers and *Hansard* reports. Although they could not be quoted in court, there was nothing to prevent Lord Denning from reading himself to sleep with *Hansard*. He was one of the first to favour the Purposive Rule, which three years ago reached its climax in the case of *Pepper v Hart* when six Law Lords outvoted the present Lord Chancellor in deciding that, where legislation is ambiguous or obscure, or leads to uncertainty, the court may try to discover the intention of Parliament by referring to the speeches of ministers or others who piloted the Act in either House of Parliament. None of the Law Lords who decided that had ever had to pilot a Bill. If they had, they would have known that in doing so one often had to change one's mind on particular clauses, or even on a principle, in order to get the Bill passed. So *Hansard* inevitably contains contradictions or ambiguous statements by those responsible. How much better it would be to make the drafting clear, so as to avoid consulting *Hansard*! *Pepper v Hart* causes the work of the courts and of barristers to be longer and more expensive, and will one day be superseded.

There is still a growing concern over the complexity of our statutes, especially those which affect the rights and duties of the citizens. Those statutes which dealt with constitutional matters in the distant past and in the recent past were well-drafted in broad terms and were expressed as matters of principle. They are well understood and have scarcely ever given rise to problems of interpretation.

The Future

What are we to do to persuade the powers that be to improve matters? How are we to convince the government of the day, whatever its politics, the ladies and gentlemen in Whitehall, how are we to convince the Members of Parliament? Don't worry about the Lords! Ours is mainly a Revising Chamber and for some years we have found it necessary to make about 2 000 amendments a session to Bills sent to us by the Commons, many of them made to improve drafting.

Lest you think my approach has so far been too negative, I now venture to put forward some constructive proposals for improving our statute laws in future:

1   Governments should allow much more time for the preparation of major Bills, preferably two years, so that the draftsman is not rushed and so that there is enough time for thorough consultation with outside experts.
2   The Law Commission, which is making a great effort to simplify statute law, should be asked to consider many more of the Government's proposals to legislate and to publish a draft Bill on each one.
3   Since we do not have a system of scrutiny of Bills by an independent body of experts, like they do in France with the *Conseil d'Etat*, it would here be a real advantage if the Law Commission were also to be asked to consider other Bills before they are published.
4   Some matters should be excluded altogether from primary legislation:

   (i)   Unenforceable provisions: including these results in the enactment of 'a dead letter'.
   (ii)   Matters relating solely to the internal administration of government, such as requiring departmental ministers to consult the Treasury.
   (iii)   Directions for controlling the procedures of public bodies. These are best contained in secondary legislation.
   (iv)   Although detailed provisions are necessary to define people's rights and duties in fiscal and some other legislation (and should often be preceded by statements of principle), attempts to cover separately every hypothetical circumstance should be avoided.

5   In recent years unavoidable details, instead of being written into a statute have sometimes been included in Codes of Practice (as in the Employment Act 1980 and the Police and Criminal Evidence Act 1984). This is justifiable when the Codes are approved by Parliament.
6   The intention of Parliament should be expressed, making full use of statement of principle or of purpose; it must not be left to be inferred from a mass of detail. The EU requires the reasons for each legislative instrument to be expressed in its preamble, and that is helpful although we would put them in clauses.

One could put forward many more suggestions but in my opinion those I have mentioned would be the most helpful steps to take. Perhaps I should add that we should try to do more to 'educate our masters', who are now the members of the House of Commons. If they were prepared to trust the courts, hypothetical details in legislation could be replaced by statements of principle. Our Parliament spends more time discussing legislation than any other Parliament in the world.

Conclusion

Legislation which cannot be understood even by experts, or which is of uncertain legal effect, brings the law into contempt and with it the Parliament which makes it. This is a disservice to democracy. It blurs and weakens the rights of the individual. It eases the way for wrongdoers and places honest people at the mercy of the state. We must all try to do better.

3 Statutory Interpretation in Labour Law*

Roger Rideout

Introduction

Two main streams of labour law, individual and collective, may be thought to be two completely separate subjects. Certainly in these days they are usually taught as such. The inevitable interaction between collective bargaining, of which industrial action is one step, and the employment relationship governed by contract, cannot disguise the complete separation of legislation relating to industrial relations and trade union power and legislation relating to individual employment rights. Nevertheless, the same courts interpret both sets of legislation and both ultimately relate to the same relationship. It would be reasonable, therefore, to expect an underlying attitude to interpretation to be applied in both cases. It is suggested that this principle is the normal judicial preference for individualism as against collectivism. But it is also suggested that legal concept is allowed to produce the assumption that the employer is an individual and the only collective is a trade union. Whatever retreat there has been during this century, and especially recently, from the attitude which provoked the development of the tort of conspiracy, there can be little question that the courts are opposed to collective power. What was once thought to be the normal judicial approach in the United Kingdom of non-interference in industrial relations has been revealed, since the late 1950s, as a temporary departure from the traditional approach of limitation of collective power. As Wedderburn[1] says

> the areas of judicial 'creativity', of new doctrines hostile to trade union interests, have been largely, though not entirely, co-terminus with the periods of British social history in which trade unions have been perceived by middle class opinion as a threat to the established order ... The lack of such 'creativity' by the

17

courts in the 1930s can similarly be related to the extreme weakness of trade unions in that decade.

It is, of course, entirely true that the period of legislative non-intervention is much longer than that covered by the period of inter-war depression. The period of judicial inaction in the collective area extends beyond the 1930s. It seems that the courts were prepared to take a lead from the legislature after 1906. It is suggested, however, that Lord Wedderburn's inference that judicial non-intervention would not have survived as long as it did but for the depression (and it may be added the intervention of the Second World War) is justified.

It is suggested that the same preference for individualism colours the approach to individual employment law. This may seem inevitable but in fact the lawyer's approach to the employment relationship, founded on the concept of an individual contract, permits the courts to ignore the fact that the employment relationship is essentially a matter of collective organization. Constant reference to 'the employer' is apparently sufficient to conceal the fact that, save in the case of small companies having very little influence on the general structure of terms and conditions, management is a collective force. The employee, unless alone in a small company, is treated as one of a group. The concept of a contract enables the lawyer to sustain his faith in two myths, namely, that in some way the existence of a contract maintains equality, and that the parties are acting as individuals. These self-deceptions permit the inherent dislike of collectives free operation when the courts are dealing with industrial relations in the same way as they permit the courts to ignore the economic power of one party when dealing with individual employment rights. The employer does not change his approach whenever it conflicts with the reality of the industrial situation. 'He' is able to manipulate the individual contract more or less as he wishes. For reasons which are not the subject of this chapter the courts have, in any event, tilted that contract in favour of the employer.

So the employer is able, today, to talk of 'individualizing' the contract. The Government welcomes and fosters that approach and that approach further reinforces the dislike of overtly collective intervention. This approach has already been described as a total deceit. But both Government and employer see collective labour as a threat. They find instinctive support in the courts which traditionally protect individual rights. If it is true that this natural instinct was artificially diverted between the wars then it is not surprising that there was a pent-up desire to re-assert the inherent individual approach. The purpose of this chapter is to show that the desire has a significant effect on the judicial approach to statutory interpretation in both principal aspects of labour law.

Although it has been suggested that the courts may have accepted a legislative lead towards non-intervention, it was the courts that led the way out of that policy. It may well be that the explanation is that the period of non-intervention was no more than one of lack of opportunity. There is no evidence that employers sought to control industrial action by resort to the courts between the wars. It may well be they, rather than the employer, who took a lead from the legislative declaration of 1906. Until at least the 1970s any consideration of individual rights would have, almost always, manifested itself in the context of a claim arising from termination of the contract of employment. Such claims were relatively few and reported decisions almost a rarity. The phase of non-intervention appears rather to have spent itself than to have ended with any change of heart.

Collective Action

The Developing Scene

So far as the legislature is concerned Davies and Freedland[2] have shown that Governments of both parties during the 1960s became progressively less committed to the concept of partnership with trade unions. It was a Labour Government which produced *In Place of Strife*[3] reversing many of the assumptions of the Donovan Commission.[4] Shortly afterwards, a Conservative Government produced the Industrial Relations Act 1971 in an attempt to introduce regulation into voluntary bargaining. In 1971 there still existed considerable public support for the position of trade unions. Without it the total rejection by the trade union movement of the philosophy of regulation would not have succeeded. It seems probable that it was the success of that total rejection and the fact that repeal of the 1971 legislation left the trade unions in an apparently unchallengeable position which strengthened judicial instinct into resolve to counter a lack of legislative control. The Master of the Rolls said during a tour of Canada in 1979, that the forthcoming general election was 'all about union power'. It is, however, impossible to understand the extent to which the judiciary was able, by restrictive interpretation of the statutory 'immunities' afforded to trade unions, effectively to develop a judicial policy of intervention in industrial relations without some consideration of the development of a basis for collective liability. It is also suggested that the two strands sprang from one policy.

Most significantly it is necessary briefly to outline the development of the principal weapon which statutory immunity has been designed to render ineffective. Until the decision of the House of Lords in *D.C. Thomson and Company Limited v Deakin*[5] only the direct form of the tort of inducement to breach of contract had been applied to industrial disputes. That is to say, the liability of strike organizers was seen to spring from the attack on the contracts of employment of the strikers. The existing statutory immunity,[6] assuming it applied to specific heads of tort liability, was confined to attacks on the contract of employment. Historically there is something to be said for this limitation since the tort recognized by *Lumley v Gye*[7] was itself a lineal descendent of the action for enticement of a servant and Crompton J. had specifically relied on that form of liability. Jenkins L.J. considered that interference with other contractual relationships had been recognized as actionable in *Quinn v Leathem*,[8] but that decision was in the context of conspiracy.[9] As is well known, the House of Lords, in *Thomson v Deakin*, was able to conceal the application of the tort of inducement to commercial contract and its extension to a vital indirect form, behind the principle, derived from *Allen v Flood*,[10] which excluded liability for advocating a lawful act merely because the means of achieving it might have been unlawful. The actual decision in that case was that the trade union organizer was not liable for the tort of inducement to breach of contract because no breach of the contract of employment had ever occurred. Nevertheless, the decision established, as essential elements of the indirect form of the tort, intention, the need for the use of unlawful means, and the existence of knowledge of the contract breach of which formed the subject of the action. In the direct form, moreover, the contracting party subject to the inducement would be unable to sue since either he had resisted the inducement so that no loss arose or he had caused his own loss by yielding to the inducement.

It may well have seemed to the House of Lords that the tort that had been recognized in this case was sufficiently constrained to be unlikely to threaten the legality of industrial action. Even if the strike organizer had advocated the use of unlawful means it would probably at that time have been assumed that immunity could successfully have been claimed under section 3 of the Trade Disputes Act 1906. It should also be borne in mind that at that time it was far from clear that strike action would be regarded as inevitably constituting a breach of the contract of employment. In *South Wales Miners Federation v Glamorgan Coal Company*[11] the breach was seen to be produced by the unusual circumstances that the collective agreement, incorporated into the individual contracts of employment, expressly forbade the giving of notice save on the last day of the month. Recognition of the fact that industrial action does involve a breach of the contract of employment is the essential link to liability in the tort of inducement. That link was first effectively fashioned by Lord Devlin in *Rookes v Barnard*.[12] It was endorsed by the Donovan Report[13] and survived the doubts expressed by Lord Denning in *Morgan v Fry*,[14] reappearing with full force in *Simmons v Hoover Limited*.[15] Subsequently this essential illegality was extended to almost all forms of industrial action.[16] Unaware of these impending developments the House of Lords might also have thought that there was some scope to develop justification as a defence in industrial dispute situations.[17] Finally, the House might have comforted itself with the thought that if the extended tort did threaten industrial action it could be confined by statute to particular examples of breach. Alternatively, of course, the House might have been conscious of the fact that, behind a screen of non-liability, it was perfecting the principal weapon against industrial action.

As it happened, none of these supposed safeguards proved reliable. There never was any legislative attempt to restrict the tort to particular situations. The defence of justification was never developed and, by far the most significant factor, the courts steadily whittled away the limiting essential elements defined in *Thomson's case*. Finally, the tort was to be extended to interference less than inducement to breach.[18] The most interesting aspect of these developments in the tort and contract approach, from the point of view of a paper on statutory interpretation, are that they took place simultaneously with the development of a new-found judicial restrictiveness towards the 1906 statutory 'immunity'. The two paths entwined at a time of intense public interest in the problem of industrial action. There can be little doubt that the whittling away of the restrictions on tort liability and the attack on legislative immunity developed from a judicial desire to control industrial action. Most significant among the extensions of tort liability was the virtual elimination of the requirement of knowledge of the contract. Imputed knowledge was accepted as sufficient in *J.T. Stratford v Lindley*[19] and *Emerald Construction Company Limited v Lowthian*.[20] Lord Denning himself admitted that the element of knowledge was virtually non-existent in a situation where the extended tort of *interference* with contract applied.[21]

Restriction of Statutory Immunity

Up to this point in time the courts had relied more on the extension of tort liability to bypass statutory immunity than upon a head-on attack on the scope of the legislation by restrictive interpretation. The exception to this was the early frontal assault in the case of *Rookes v Barnard*[22] in which the House of Lords had not only developed the tort of intimidation outside the reach of statutory immunity[23] but had also suggested that actions rendered immune by statute might continue to form the unlawful element necessary for indirect liability for inducement of breach of contract. This argument, as we shall see, revived with the repeal of an extension of statutory immunity to cover that consequence by schedule 4 of the Employment Act 1982 which Henry J. accepted in *Barretts and Baird (Wholesalers) Limited v IPCS*[24] as making it possible again to say that a breach, though immune, constituted an unlawful act. The possibility was not finally disposed of until the decision of the House of Lords in *Hadmor Productions Limited v Hamilton*[25] by which time the courts had good reason to suppose that the legislature was again intent on control.

A whole-hearted attack on statutory immunity seems to have been prompted largely by the enactment in 1976 (Trade Union and Labour Relations Act) of what proved to be the high point of statutory immunity extending immunity to all interference with contract and, incidentally, specifically eliminating the chance of employing immune actions as unlawful elements. The attack was led by Lord Denning who, a few years earlier in resisting Sir John Donaldson's interpretation of the 1971 Act, had appeared as something of a champion of trade unions. It was most strongly resisted by Lord Scarman who, in *MWL v Woods*[26] said, 'the law now is back to what Parliament had intended when it enacted the Act of 1906 – but stronger and clearer than it was then.' He made his policy plain in *Express Newspapers Limited v McShane*[27] where he said, 'it would need very clear statutory language' to persuade him that 'Parliament intended to allow the Court to act as some sort of back seat driver in trade disputes'. Lord Diplock, who also resisted the restrictive interpretations of the Court of Appeal, had a very different purpose in mind. In *Duport Steels Limited v Sirs*[28] he said that statutory immunities are 'intrinsically repugnant to anyone who has spent his life in the practice of the law'. For him their effects 'have tended to stick in judicial gorges'.

The story of the restrictive interpretation of the 'golden formula' of the Trade Disputes Act 1906 was told many times as it unfolded. The legislation of the 1980s so completely made the purpose of such interpretation obsolete that it has rarely been told in detail since and will bear some repetition now.

The total immunity afforded to trade unions as such in 1906 appeared so complete and impenetrable that little attempt was ever made effectively to limit it at any time before its repeal in 1982.[29] Since its repeal it has been revealed as a locked door behind which lay the power to sequestrate union funds following refusal to comply with an injunction forbidding industrial action. This power is such as to render the trade union virtually impotent in the further direction and financing of the industrial action. Since the repeal, courts have gone so far as to develop the injunction to the point of giving instructions to the union to take positive steps to prevent continuation of industrial action and the legislature has endorsed such a requirement. It is, perhaps, surprising that more attempt was not made to find a weak point in this trade union immunity since even when individual immunity has been broken down individual liability has a limited effect on the cessation of industrial action. Coupled with legislative reduction in the scope of immunity the opening of trade union liability has produced a situation in which there can scarcely be said to be a semblance of the 'right to strike' which Lord Denning thought he saw in the decision in *Morgan v Fry*.[30]

More than any other legislative measure in the 1980s, exposure of trade unions to liability rendered the judicial attack no longer necessary. The courts, however, finding union immunity unassailable, concentrated on the lesser immunity which had been offered to individual organizers of industrial action. The attack centred on three aspects of the formulation of statutory immunity:

(a)   its limitation to specific torts;
(b)   the existence of a trade dispute; and
(c)   'Action in contemplation or furtherance' of that dispute.

Limitation to specific torts   Fiercely as Lord Wedderburn, in particular, might rail against the outcome, resistance to the conclusion in *Rookes v Barnard*[31] that the Trade Disputes Act 1906, section 3, only applied to the torts of conspiracy (in the form which *Crofter Hand Woven Harris Tweed Company v Veitch*[32] rendered of little practical effect against industrial action) and inducement to breach of contract of employment, was hopeless from the outset. The daily accounts of the arguments in *Rookes* reveal that only slowly did the tort of intimidation emerge as a support to the original claim of conspiracy to commit an unlawful act. It was said at the time that Salmond, in 1909, had conjured the tort of intimidation out of the early conspiracy cases. There is much in the language of section 3 to support the view that it was all intended to refer to specific heads of tort liability and it would be very surprising if one sub-section clearly so referred whilst the next referred generally to the consequences of action. Only such an interpretation would have been capable of applying section 3 to liability for intimidation.

With hindsight it can clearly be seen that the Attorney-General, Dilke, would have been better advised to devise a blanket immunity such as he provided for trade unions. It seems very unlikely that he saw his task at the time as extending beyond rendering ineffective those heads of tort liability which had been developed and which appeared to threaten industrial action. The fact that intimidation is a very dangerous tort in this respect because it breaks through privity of contract, so as to allow action to third parties such as Rookes, cannot be used in retrospect to suggest a legislative intention that did not exist. Specific immunity from liability for intimidation was granted by statute in 1976 and survives to the present time.[33] Somewhat surprisingly this immunity has not subsequently been attacked and the tort of intimidation has not again appeared as a major weapon against industrial action.[34]

The existence of a trade dispute   The attack on the scope of 'trade dispute' was not mounted until the late 1970s. By then considerable detail had been added, first by the Trade Union and Labour Relations Act 1974[35] which was, in turn, significantly restricted in 1982.[36] Before the words 'a dispute between workers and their employers' were added in 1982 the trade union could raise a dispute on its own initiative, regardless of support from employees who were the subject of the dispute;[37] and before the insertion of the words 'wholly or mainly' it was only necessary to find *some* connection between the action and 'trade' elements in the definition.[38] At this stage, therefore, Lord Denning led the Court of Appeal in a more general attack upon the concept of furtherance which had not previously engaged much attention.

In *Express Newspapers Limited v McShane*[39] the dispute concerning pay was between the proprietors of local newspapers and journalists employed by them. The National Union of Journalists called a strike and requested journalists employed by the Press Association, which supplied copy both to local and national newspapers, to join the strike action. There was no dispute involving national newspapers. The union also called on its members working for national newspapers, including those owned by the plaintiffs, to refuse to use Press Association material.

The Court of Appeal held that in order for an act to be in contemplation or furtherance of a trade dispute it must be reasonably capable, or have a practical prospect of, furthering the dispute. In its view two primary elements were necessary: (a) a genuine intention to achieve the objective of the dispute, and (b) action which was reasonably capable of achieving that objective. The action must give practical, and not merely moral, support to one side or the other. 'Furtherance is not a merely subjective concept. There is an objective element to it.'

Paradoxically, this piece of constructive interpretation would have been more convincing if it could have been said that contemplation or furtherance should be read together but Lord Denning had firmly separated them by holding that contemplation ceased once the dispute had matured to the point of furtherance. It might have been said by the same court in another situation that if the legislature had intended this result it could easily have said so.

The House of Lords was unanimous in concluding that the action in question was in furtherance of the dispute but a majority rejected the requirement of objective furtherance, holding that all that was necessary was that the person doing the act does so with the purpose of helping a party to the dispute to achieve its objective, honestly and reasonably believing that his act will so assist. Lord Wilberforce, in the minority, considered this interpretation a hybrid and said that there was a stark choice between an objective test and a subjective test which looked only to the stated purpose of the actor. He then came down in favour of an even more uncertain hybrid which involved an 'objective element' looked at 'in the light of the evidence, giving due weight, but not conclusive force, to the genuine belief of those who initiate the action in question'.[40] Lord Diplock pointed out the blindingly obvious, which had undoubtedly been in the mind of the Court of Appeal, that the objective test would give the court the right to substitute its own opinion for that of the trade union. But his expression of repugnance at such a conclusion can scarcely have been other than a plea to a now sympathetic government. The legislative change took effect almost immediately after this decision.[41]

The Legislature Joins the Courts

The period during which the courts had apparently stood alone in defence of economic interest against what was widely seen as the selfish pressure of trade union power and industrial action was over. Nevertheless, some courts continued to sharpen old, and fashion new, weapons of the common law *ex abundante cautela*. A new tort of interference with trade was fashioned from the continuing development of the tort of inducement to breach of contract, possibly with an eye to reintroduction of legislative protection at a later date.[42] In *Merkur Island Shipping Corporation v Laughton*[43] the House of Lords took the opportunity to approve the development of the tort of *interference* with contract, so long championed by Lord Denning. In *Mead v Haringey LBC*[44] Lord Denning set about fashioning the tort of inducement to breach of statutory duty, 'confident', he said, 'that the people at large would have supported such a move'. The long miners' strike in 1984 permitted the courts to equate the contract of membership of a trade union with the very vires of the union itself so as to prevent the conduct of a strike in breach of that contract as being beyond the powers of the union.[45] In *Thomas v NUM (South Wales Area)*[46] the court sought to invent a tort of 'unreasonable harassment' to deal with picketing.

But already, in *The Universal Sentinel*,[47] Lord Diplock was content to leave the development of legislative policy to the legislature. Although the statutory immunities did not directly apply to a ship-owner's action for money had and received as a result of economic duress by a trade union, he said that he saw

> an indication, which your Lordships should respect, of where public policy requires that the line should be drawn between what kind of commercial pressure by a trade union upon an employer in the field of industrial relations ought to be treated as legitimised despite the fact that the will of the employer is thereby coerced.

As Lord Goff put it, 'an action of restitution [may] by rejected as inconsistent with a policy of [the] statute.' One might be forgiven for thinking that the legislative indicators were rather more clearly against the development of more tortious liability in industrial relations in 1964 than they were in 1982. The difference in judicial approach appears only to be explicable on the basis of the change of legislative policy from defence of union action to attack upon it. Far from responding to legislative policy, it is suggested that the courts have consistently pursued their own.

Perhaps the clearest declaration that the war was over and open hostilities should cease appears in the decision of the House of Lords in *Hadmor Productions v Hamilton*.[48] Lord Denning in the Court of Appeal[49] had contended that the repeal of section 13(3) of the 1974 Act (which had stated that 'for the avoidance of doubt' an act given statutory immunity could not constitute the unlawful element in indirect interference with contract) by Section 17 of the Employment Act 1980 could not have been intended to leave the issue in doubt again and must, therefore, be read as intended to indicate that immune torts could constitute unlawful means.

To reach this conclusion he took account of parliamentary history to an extent never before, or since, attempted by an English court. The examination forced him to admit that had section 13(3) remained it would have provided immunity for the secondary 'blacking' of goods; but he failed to admit that that was the more likely reason for the repeal. If Lord Denning felt able to support this conclusion by an extensive survey of parliamentary history it seems only fair that criticism of it may be suggested by his own history. It seems very unlikely that the extremely cautious approach that section 17 of the Employment Act 1980 took would have satisfied his obvious objectives in the series of decisions leading up to it. It is just possible, therefore, that he was continuing to fight the war.

Lord Diplock, delivering the only judgment of the House of Lords, may have been aware that in future little would turn upon the scope of section 17. The Government had declared its position and the war would be won by legislation, little by little. He pointed out that Lord Denning's 'doubt' was actually a feeling that the suggestion might be wrong at common law. Common sense supports his conclusion that Parliament cannot be supposed to have intended to resurrect the issue. Section 13(3) was otiose. It had been repealed simply to stop it getting in the way of withdrawal of immunity of secondary action.

Action in contemplation or furtherance   The new legislative policy towards restrictive immunity was unlikely to attract the same hostile interpretation as had accompanied the old. No step was taken to reverse the approach of the House of Lords to the question of contemplation or furtherance of a trade dispute. Instead it was provided that trade disputes must in future be between workers and *their* employer. Trade disputes could in future only arise when they wholly or mainly concerned one of the specified industrial headings. In a sense this might be seen as a vote of confidence in the courts because it plainly conferred a discretion upon them as to when a primary purpose was established.

In *Mercury Communications Limited v Scott-Garner*[50] Mercury had been given permission to operate a private telecommunication system. The then Post Office Engineering Union, objecting to this precursor to ultimate privatization, instructed its members to refuse to connect Mercury's system to the British Telecommunications Network. The union sought to differentiate its political from its industrial purposes by asserting that its object was to 'prevent the risk of job losses arising from the entry into the market of an unwelcome competitor'. May L.J. came to the conclusion that the real dispute was between the union and the Government and industrial action a bargaining counter therein. If the union was bargaining with the Government it can scarcely have realistically supposed it was bargaining to drop the policy of privatization. It must surely have been bargaining for the introduction into that policy of protective measures for its members. It is suggested that the dispute was plainly about the terms and conditions of the union members and their future prospects. This may well, of course, not have constituted a dispute between the workers and their employer, but that is another matter. As Kahn-Freund asked,[51] is it not true that most major industrial problems will arise from the effects of government policy in one form or another?

The ultimate decision would seem then to be one of approach and this might be sought to be borne out by the decision in *Associated British Ports v GTWU*.[52] The Government proposed to abolish the national Dock Labour Scheme which, *inter alia*, would have localized any collective bargaining which survived the destruction of the grip on employment which that scheme effectively gave the unions. Three of the largest registered employers sought interlocutory injunctions to restrain threatened strike action, alleging that the dispute was political and aimed at the Government, and that a strike would be a breach of each employee's statutory duty to be available for work. Millet J. concluded that there was no foundation for the contention that the dispute was political and that it was impossible to contend that the union had manufactured a spurious trade dispute. The conclusion that the strike would be in furtherance of a dispute concerning the immediate, direct and serious impact of abolition on terms and conditions was in his view 'inescapable'.

It is interesting that this aspect of his judgment was not challenged in the subsequent appeal. Was it, indeed, recognized that the courts were likely to exercise their discretion in this way in a situation where the dockers had already lost in any event? The only effect of a strike would be further to enhance the success of non-scheme ports and outside depots. Adherence to the scheme would have led inevitably to rapid decline of the port concerned. There was nothing in the short, let alone in the long, term to gain and the strike was no more than a gesture of protest. It is submitted that nothing in this decision supports any suggestion of a weakening in the position taken in *Dimbleby and Sons Limited v NUJ*[53] that a trade union can no longer turn a political dispute into a trade dispute by introducing a claim for a term excluding politically objectionable conditions.

That case, incidentally, demonstrates the effectiveness of diversification by the employer of his operations between various companies. A dispute over allocation of work, it was held, would cease to be a trade dispute the moment an employer decided to allocate work from one group of employees to a group employed by another company. In this instance the second company was not a wholly-owned subsidiary of the first, but it would have made no difference if it had been. No criticism is levelled at this interpretation. The careful differentiation in section 17 of the 1980 Employment Act between associated and non-associated employers indicates that the legislature was wholly aware of the effect of the corporate veil. Once again the indication is clear that the courts can safely relax. The legislature has reasserted its control over trade union power.

Associated Legislation

Dismissal during Industrial Action

Dismissal of those engaged in industrial action is a formidable weapon if it can be deployed. Deployment depends on how readily the employer can replace those dismissed and maintain production. The advent of a non-contractual criterion of reasonableness governing the legitimacy of dismissal posed a problem of potential restriction of the employer's power to dismiss in such a situation. Fascinating as would have been the consequences of restrospective arbitration by the courts on the merits of the dispute, it is scarcely surprising that the legislature discarded the option of permitting the courts to decide the issue of reasonableness of dismissal in such circumstances.

Withdrawal from the arena, which was the preferred solution, left managerial prerogative to fire free to operate and could be said to work wholly in favour of the employer rather than being an example of neutrality as claimed. The legislature appears to have acknowledged this originally by forcing the

employer to meet the collective force of labour head on.[54] But that 'equal-
izer' was repealed[55] and the employer was allowed selectively to re-engage
at any time more than three months after the dismissal. In addition, the
requirement that the employer should face collective force was modified to
provide that the employer need only act non-discriminatorily between those
continuing to take the industrial action at the time of dismissal. Ten years
later[56] all protection against victimization was removed for those participat-
ing in unofficial industrial action. The original purpose of no victimization
seems to have been acknowledged by the courts in the decision in *Frank
Jones (Tipton) Limited v Stock.*[57]

In *Williams v National Theatre Board Limited*[58] a sympathizer with the
strikers was dismissed along with them for fear that failure to dismiss her
after she had returned to work would destroy the employer's immunity from
claims for unfair dismissal. Subsequently, however, she was re-engaged on
precisely the same terms as she had before dismissal. All the other strikers,
however, were offered re-engagement on condition that they would be treated
as having received a second warning, in effect placing them at risk of
summary dismissal for a wide range of relatively minor offences.

Lord Denning interpreted the statutory reference to re-engagement in the
same job as ensuring only the same job capacity. In his view the section did
not preclude the attachment of different terms and conditions. He anticipated, not for the first time, impending legislative change. The limitations
on the use of dismissal as a weapon were to be reduced in very much the
same way as immunities from liability for industrial action were reduced. It
did not seem to matter to Lord Denning that he could not define what he
meant by 'capacity' save by a series of selective examples of what he called
the attachment of 'unreasonable' strings. Effectively, he reduced the prohibition on victimization so as to permit selective action short of dismissal
unless the court considered that action too extreme. It is impossible to
believe that those involved in the legislative process to that time intended
such a result. As if to make his purpose clear there is no element of neutrality in Lord Denning's approach. He branded strikers as those who, by
disloyal, fundamental breach of their contract had inflicted heavy loss on
their employer.[59]

The neutrality provision did not seek to define which types of industrial
action would be excluded from the supervision of industrial tribunals. In
Faust v Power Packing Casemakers Limited[60] Stephenson L.J., while acknowledging the error in the conclusion of May J. in the court below that
the definition of 'other industrial action' could safely be left to the good
sense of an industrial tribunal (which, incidentally, that learned judge
directed to a number of wholly irrelevant considerations), said,

I feel ... no certainty as to the intention of the legislature in enacting this provision.

In threading my way from sections and sub-sections to schedules and paragraphs, and from schedule back to section, I may have lost the way, or the thread, or sight of Parliament's aim and object, even if Parliament itself did not. But of this I have no doubt, that there is no compelling reason why the words of the provision should not be given their natural and ordinary meaning, and good reason why they should not now be defined as once they were [that is to say, as involving a breach of contract].

To put it another way, there is no compelling reason to suppose that the legislature intended to preserve a right of resort from dismissal to an industrial tribunal for those who had committed no breach of obligation to their employer. It is very difficult to suppose that the courts are here adopting anything but the same restrictive approach to the freedom to strike which characterized their interpretation of immunity from tort liability.

The jurisdiction of an industrial tribunal is restored[61] if it is shown that one or more relevant employees has not been dismissed. But there is no indication of the time at which this enquiry should be made. In *P. & O. European Ferries (Dover) Limited v Byrne*[62] the Court of Appeal, overruling both the industrial tribunal and the EAT, held that the proper construction required one to look at the end of the tribunal proceedings – its final 'determination'. This reasoning was based on the fact that the lifting of the prohibition on making a 'determination' must relate to a decision. If this is, as May L.J. said, the 'clear and plain meaning' it permits the employer to obtain disclosure of the identity of those alleged to have been retained in employment and to dismiss them thus providing a bar to further industrial tribunal proceedings. It is not surprising that May L.J. described the opposite construction as 'purposive'. But he seems, thereby, to admit that interpretation of the provision is not to be made in the light of its clear intention to exclude discrimination.

Action Short of Dismissal

Until the legislature cast doubt on such a conclusion in 1993 by enacting a restrictive interpretation by the Court of Appeal there would seem to have been little room for doubt that the purpose of the Trade Union and Labour Relations (Consolidation) Act 1992, section 146, was to protect an employee from victimization for trade union membership, non-membership or activities.[63] This provision originated in the Industrial Relations Act 1971, section 5 of which had made it an unfair industrial practice to discriminate on grounds of union membership and had specifically referred to the imposition of penalties. A provision similar to that in the 1992 Act was enacted in the Employment Protection Act 1975 and consolidated into the 1978 Act.[64] Because the 1975 Act had contained no definition of 'action' it could not be defined in the Consolidating Act.[65]

In *Post Office v Crouch*[66] the House of Lords, somewhat surprisingly, had taken a very wide view of the protection afforded by holding that action against the union was action against each member. The words 'as an individual' had been introduced to restrict this construction. But in *National Coal Board v Ridgway*[67] the Court of Appeal had held the denial of a wage rise to members of one trade union affected them individually and so was within the meaning of Section 23 (1) of the 1978 Act if its purpose was to penalize or deter union membership. Specifically, 'action' included omission despite the fact that there was no provision to this effect and a 1971 reference to exclusion from benefits had not been re-enacted in 1975.

A similar point arose both in *Wilson v Associated Newspapers Limited* and *Palmer v Associated British Ports*[68] but, significantly, by the time the Court of Appeal considered the case the Government, in a Green Paper, had announced its intention of reversing the decision in *Ridgway* and, by the time the House of Lords made its decision, it had done so. As we have seen several times in this chapter this is a not untypical example of reason for a change in judicial interpretation of *existing* labour legislation in the light of an anticipated change in legislative policy.

In *Wilson's case* the employers gave notice to terminate current collective agreements and withdraw recognition from the National Union of Journalists. Only journalists agreeing to the new 'individual' contract would be given a pay rise. They were, however, free to remain members of the union. The EAT held that the purpose of the employer was to end collective bargaining rather than deter membership of a trade union.

Palmer was employed by Associated British Ports, which had recognized the National Union of Rail, Maritime and Transport Workers. He was asked to relinquish representation by his union and accept a contract the terms of which were not collectively negotiated, in return for higher basic and overtime rates. Employees who refused this offer continued to be represented by the union, which retained the right to negotiate on their behalf, but their pay settlement in 1991 was substantially lower than the rise offered to those who accepted non-representation. The EAT concluded that the employer's purpose was to achieve individual flexibility. Individual contracts were the means of doing so.

In both cases, therefore, the EAT had not concerned itself with statutory interpretation but had reached decisions contrary to those of the industrial tribunals by way of its own conclusion as to the employer's purpose. The Court of Appeal allowed the employees' appeals in both cases. It rejected the distinction between union membership and use of the services of a union, following its earlier decision that if this were the correct approach the section would be worthless since it would only preserve bare union membership with none of the specific advantages which make that attractive. The Court of Appeal also rejected the attempt of the EAT in *Palmer's case* to distinguish between a purpose and a means of achieving it. Intention and motive may be distinguishable[69] but purpose applies to both. In the view of Dillon L.J., it could properly be said to be both the employer's purpose to persuade employees to abandon union representation and to cause union membership to fall away. The effect of *Ridgway* and of the Court of Appeal decisions in *Wilson* and *Palmer*, therefore, is that whilst an employer is free to bargain or refuse to bargain he cannot offer benefits to those who support his purpose, denying those benefits to those who do not, without discriminating contrary to the statutory prohibition.

It was not until the presentation of arguments to the House of Lords that it was contended that 'action' did not include omission. In this respect, of course, the Court of Appeal would have been bound by its previous decision in *Ridgway*. A majority of the House of Lords took the view that it was not possible to substitute the word 'omission' for 'action' (as section 153 (1) of the 1992 Act provided) in the phrase 'the right not to have action ... taken against him'. This conclusion seems questionable. Section 153 talks of the context, not the grammatical construction, and it is often the case that substitution of a positive for a negative, or some similar provision, in such a section requires some minor grammatical revision.

Because of that grammatical difficulty the House considered that it was entitled to look at the parliamentary history to ascertain whether the phrase should be re-written to include the word 'omission'. In the view of the majority it must have been apparent to those responsible for drafting the 1975 Act that its predecessor had specifically included denial of benefits. Nevertheless, they omitted to specify anything but 'action'. The omission of the draftsman could not be explained by taking account of the likely intention of a Labour Government, but it is submitted that, since the whole House agreed that the purpose of the statutory provision was to outlaw discrimination, Parliament could not have intended only to apply the protection to adverse acts and not to exclusion of benefits. It must be self-evident that it would be easy for a discriminator to substitute benefit for one side for penalty to the other.

If the majority turned to the parliamentary history because the words of the Act left them in doubt it is strange that their enquiry should have chosen to stop at an equally inconclusive point in the possible explanation of the mind of the legislature. Lord Browne-Wilkinson was obviously unhappy and did no more than declare that he was satisfied that the parliamentary history made it impossible to conclude that section 153 was intended to apply to section 23

(1). He felt compelled to accept, as had the strict constructionist, Lord Bridge, that the effective parliamentary history began not in 1971 but in 1975. Lord Bridge found it inconceivable that if the draftsman had wanted to achieve as wide coverage he should not have used similar language. There are, of course, several reasons why, in the aftermath of repeal of the Industrial Relations Act of 1971, the legislature should not wish to see adopted the same words as had protected members of in-house unions. Nor, having resorted to parliamentary history to explain words otherwise not clear, is it entirely convincing for Lord Bridge to justify his admittedly 'literalistic' construction by saying that, as the courts look at the ordinary grammatical meaning of words, so parliamentary draftsmen use language with the utmost precision. Clearly, the draftsman had not done so in this case. The context, it is submitted, did not preclude reading 'action' to include 'omission'.

With some reservation from Lord Slynn, the House unanimously preferred the view of 'purpose' adopted by the EAT to that of the Court of Appeal. This may be expressed as a conclusion that, having eliminated collective bargaining, the employer did not care whether union membership withered or flourished. Thus to conclude would be to say that concerted industrial action was likely to be ineffective unless it is combined with access to collective bargaining. The employer's freedom to terminate collective bargaining arrangements will remain whilst the courts take the view that this is action against the union rather than against the individuals. But where action is taken to persuade individuals to participate in the reduction of the union's bargaining rights this is surely the sort of discriminatory action by reason of trade union activities that the legislature intended to protect the employee against. Thus, when the House of Lords goes on to say that the purpose of the statute was to protect union membership, and not to protect a non-existent right to bargain, it is confusing the right of the trade union to bargain with the right of the individual to take advantage of the product of that bargaining. It is shutting one's eyes to reality to suggest that the freedom to be a member of a trade union without discrimination is the freedom to be a member of a friendly society. The employee joins a trade union primarily so that it may bargain for him and effective protection against discrimination must be protection in respect of that function.

The House of Lords appears to have rejected the idea that an employer might have a dual purpose in taking such action. The Government did not take the same view because in 1993[70] it provided that if the evidence suggested that the employer might either intend to change his relationship with any class of worker or, alternatively, to discriminate contrary to the section, he should be presumed to have the first purpose unless no reasonable employer would have taken the action with such a purpose. Presumably, in this provision 'action' can be taken to include 'omission'.

By way of conclusion of this section it may be appropriate to cite just one further example in which the courts would appear to have adopted a more liberal interpretation once aware that the legislative approach was about to become less permissive towards collective industrial power. It concerns the restrictive judicial response to the power of ACAS to make legally binding recommendations for recognition under the Employment Protection Act.[71] Only when the Employment Act 1980[72] repealed this decision did the House of Lords hold that ACAS had a wider jurisdiction to improve industrial relations.[73]

Individual Protection

The burden of the argument of this chapter has been that the courts lean in favour of the individual, with whom they identify the employer, and against what they see as collective power. Crouch, however, took this further[74] contending that the public interest in an industrial dispute is synonymous with the employer's interest favouring the maintenance of production. In the same way as individualism also favours the preference for contractual rights so Crouch's thesis would support managerial prerogative in the maintenance of production. There are plentiful examples of this in judicial decisions. Space permits only an indication of the type of assertion to which we refer. Speaking of the definition of redundancy, Sachs L.J. said:[75]

> Similarly it does not provide for the case where an employer wishes to see if someone else can do the job better; it could indeed be industrially disastrous if it puts the brake on employers seeking to get the best man for any given job. Nor does it provide for any case where an employer simply wishes not to continue to employ a particular employee.

Similarly, Lord Denning:[76]

> an employer is entitled to reorganise his business so as to improve its efficiency and, in so doing, to propose to his staff a change in the terms and conditions of employment; and to dispense with their services if they do not agree.

Even Browne-Wilkinson J. (as he then was) said in *Rowe v Radio Rentals Ltd*:[77]

> It is very important that internal appeals procedures run by commercial companies ... should not be cramped by legal requirements imposing impossible burdens on companies in the conduct of *their personal affairs* ... in the context of these internal appeals from one man in line management to another, it must

be difficult to show that the rules of natural justice have been infringed if the person hearing the appeal in fact took the decision.

However typical may be these examples of an acceptance of management's right to manage the amount of reported support for such a view can leave no doubt that there is no judicial reluctance to rely on the terms of the contract of employment simply because it is controlled and dictated by management.[78] How courts interpret that contract[79] is not within the scope of this chapter but there is no doubt that the concepts of the law of contract have dominated judicial thought on the interpretation of individual employment legislation. As a result, the contract of employment has become much more 'visible to the naked eye of the layman' than Kahn-Freund thought it in 1954.[80] He saw that contract as 'the cornerstone of the edifice', and so it is. But he also saw it as 'one of the essential civil liberties of this country'. That, it is submitted, it certainly is not. Lord Wedderburn[81] suggests that it is better regarded as an instrument of servitude tying the worker to the convenience of the employer.

The Definition of Redundancy

Space again dictates the selection of only a few examples. The two here chosen are probably the best known applications of the concept of contract in the interpretation of employment legislation and, for that reason, will be considered by way of general reference to decisions rather than more detailed analysis of the words of the judges.

It would seem self-evident that those who interpret statutory provisions should have a view of their likely purpose even if they assert that their only object is to examine the meaning of the words. If that is so it is a pity that, to this day, no one is very clear what was the purpose of the introduction of a right to compensation for redundancy.[82] Purely pragmatically, much of the purpose was to make redundancy more readily acceptable to the worker. The payment was presented, and accepted by the courts, as compensation for the loss of accumulated skill and service. But the exclusion of any intention to provide for future loss of earning capacity has allowed acceptance to be purchased cheaply.

The statutory definition, even without judicial construction, is surprisingly narrow and leaves many workers dismissed for economic reasons unprovided for. The European Community adopted the much wider ranging provision for those dismissed for 'a reason not connected with the employee'. In consequence, as a result of compulsion to adhere to the proper interpretation of Community Directives, there exist in the United Kingdom at present two widely different concepts which, logically, ought to be ident-

ical.[83] The restricted definition of 'redundancy'[84] requires either total clo-
sure of business in the place where the employee is employed or -

> (b) the fact that the requirements of that business for employees to carry out
> work of a particular kind, or for employees to carry out work of a particular kind
> in the place where he was so employed, have ceased or diminished, or are
> expected to cease or diminish.

The judicial reluctance of United Kingdom courts to impinge on the prerogative of management has produced an insistence that tribunals must test
the decision of management rather than substituting their own judgment. In
the case of unfair dismissal that decision is tested against the standard of a
reasonable employer but in the case of redundancy the 'requirement', which
might seem to indicate the justification, is tested by no standard at all.
Speaking of this situation in which the fact of diminution normally established the requirement to do so Kilner Brown J. said:[85] 'the Act of 1974 has
taken away all the powers of courts to investigate the rights and wrongs of
industrial disputes. There is, accordingly, no power to investigate the economic justification for the employer's decision'.

A long line of early authorities seemed to leave no doubt that the place
of employment is that defined in the contract as the area in which the
employee may be required to work.[86] The categoric statements in these
cases, however, may be a confusion between the meaning of the statutory
concept of a place and the consequence of refusal to comply with a
mobility clause in a contract. The Court of Appeal in *O'Brien*[87] undoubtedly considered the situation from the standpoint taken by the industrial
tribunal that breach of the contractual obligation furnished the reason for
dismissal and prevented the employees establishing any other reason for
dismissal. The two issues are separate. Not every failure to comply with a
mobility clause will justify dismissal[88] but in *Stevenson*[89] the contractual
approach to 'place' was put in inverted commas as if it formed part of the
statutory definition.

For the first time, almost 30 years after the passing of the Redundancy
Payments Act 1965, Judge Hicks QC, whilst not disputing the reference to
the contract, contrived to place a check on the power of the employer to
dictate the course of events. In *Bass Leisure Ltd v Thomas*[90] he adopted a
strict construction of a contract which spoke of transfer from one place to
another to conclude that the transfer was to a different place of employment.
But he also showed himself aware of the confusion by pointing out separately that no breach of contract had occurred since the contract required
consideration of domestic circumstances which the EAT held should be
with a view to establishing objective suitability.

Contract permeates every aspect of interpretation of the definition. 'For the purposes for which the employee was employed' has consistently been regarded as a reference to the contactual job title or definition despite the fact that these words only occur in limb (b) of the definition. The determination of the type of work defined in the contract not only affords the employer control over redundancy situations if he wishes to draft the contract carefully but permits the courts a wide discretion if he does not or adopts too vague a description.[91] The approach varies from application of a specialized description[92] to a broad general classification.[93] The courts, furthermore, have construed out of a lack of detail in the statutory definition a further detailed requirement that only job characteristics will be considered relevant in distinguishing the jobs alleged to have diminished from those that remain.[94] The invitation to the employer to manipulate the contract on each of these issues is plain even if the result is sometimes in favour of the employee.[95]

Constructive Dismissal

When it was thought necessary, in 1965, to define dismissal as a prerequisite to a claim for redundancy compensation[96] provision was made to include the situation in which 'the employee terminates [the] contract ... in circumstances such that he is entitled to terminate it without notice by reason of the employers conduct'. When the definition of dismissal was applied to unfair dismissal in the Industrial Relations Act 1971 this aspect was not included. The present writer presumed to suggest that this omission may have been deliberate and this would seem to be confirmed by the record of the parliamentary debate.[97] The Lord Chancellor said, 'I recognise that there are cases of unfair treatment which are not covered by this clause, but this is a clause about unfair dismissal, and unfair dismissal, I fear, is where it must stop.' Deprived of this information, Sir John Donaldson, in the National Industrial Relations Court,[98] described the suggestion as mere academic pedantry.[99] He concluded, quite correctly as the law then stood, that if an employee left following a repudiatory breach by the employer he could claim at common law that the employer had terminated the contract, thereby dismissing him.[100] He caused himself and others some later difficulty in explaining why, if the dismissal occurred by reason of the employee's repudiation it could not be claimed to be no dismissal because the employee had terminated the contract. The amending Act of 1976 inserted the missing aspect which became known as 'constructive dismissal'. It was, no doubt, passed off as rectification of an omission but actually it represented a change of intention, if not by then of law, to protect the employee from employer conduct possibly deliberately designed to induce him to leave. If the contention in this chapter is correct this escapade is a rare departure from the inclination to protect the interests of the employer. This period in the career of Sir John Donaldson is rarely spoken of with approbation but it is only fair to notice a purposive construction going well beyond the legislative purpose.

The statutory repair of the omission provoked a period of startling indecision in the courts as to whether entitlement to claim a constructive dismissal arose from the unreasonable conduct of the employer or only from conduct amounting, as in Donaldson's common law insertion, from repudiatory breach.[101] The judicial obsession with contract prevailed although it is only fair to say that it is difficult to argue against the conclusion of Lord Denning that a statutory definition which speaks of *entitlement* to leave *without notice* must be referring to the consequence of repudiatory breach of contract. Once committed to the path of contract the courts developed that interpretation to its logical conclusion. They established, for example, that the employer's conduct had to be sufficiently serious to constitute a repudiation:[102] that the employee had to establish a causal connection between his leaving and the breach;[103] and that the employee must not waive the breach by failing to act sufficiently promptly.[104] Aspects of so technical a concept as repudiatory breach are a trap for the unwary lawyer and for almost all non-lawyers. It is, for example, all too easy to seek to rely on an anticipatory breach that has not occurred.[105]

Critics were relieved to observe an apparent readiness in the courts to discover implied terms breach of which produced the necessary repudiation. The most celebrated discovery was the obligation of each party to maintain the trust and confidence of the other.[106] The present writer declared general satisfaction that the worst effects of contract had been avoided[107] and the same sentiment is still, sometimes, expressed.[108] The satisfaction should have been fleeting for the Court of Appeal put an early end to any euphoria about the value of 'trust and confidence'.[109]

Neither the legislature nor the courts can be blamed for all the consequences of contract in the law of employment. Recent extension of the jurisdiction of industrial tribunals to deal with contractual issues arising on termination has exposed the vulnerability of the employee to a counterclaim in cases of alleged constructive dismissal. Should the employee fail to establish the dismissal he will, where, as will usually be the case, he has left without giving the full contractual notice, inevitably be liable to damages for breach of contract. The risk was always present but an employer was unlikely to trouble to bring a claim in a County court. The truth is that common law development of the law of the contract of employment makes it a powerful weapon in the hands of the employer. The courts have played a full part in allowing it to be unleashed as a means of controlling individual statutory provision of employee rights.

Conclusion

Analysis of so large an area as 50 years of interpretation of labour statutes is bound to be selective. It is admitted within this chapter that untypical decisions exist. Generalizations must, inevitably, be made and any statement that the judiciary adopts a certain attitude or approach is, plainly, one of them. Examples of judicial decisions favourable to collective activity in industrial disputes and to protection of the individual employee against the greatest inequalities of contract can readily be found. Nor should they be lost sight of in such an assessment of attitudes merely because they are overridden by higher courts. The decision of Browne-Wilkinson J. (as he then was) in *Woods v W.M. Car Services (Peterborough) Ltd*[110] is an example. Apparently taking the same view as the industrial tribunal and the Court of Appeal his judgment contains an entirely different assessment of the plaintiff's right to claim constructive dismissal. But it would have been dishonest to express the general assessment of judicial attitudes advanced in this chapter unless it was believed that the overwhelming weight of decisions supported it.

The thesis is that the courts in the United Kingdom have, since the end of the Second World War asserted the right of management to manage in the interests of the economy and have assisted management to resist the demand for primacy, and especially the collective demand for primacy, of the interest of the worker. During that period the attitude of Government has varied between maintaining a balance of power and releasing unregulated market forces, between employee protection and the creation of a low wage economy. In this period, however, it is submitted that the courts have been remarkably consistent in their protection of the economic interests of business, relaxing only when convinced that the legislature was actively pursuing the same policy. Should we be surprised? This is a capitalist economy. The intellectual ability of the judiciary is one of the great national assets. But it makes value judgements all the time and its values are those of capitalism, not, generally speaking, of socialism. The socialist ideal of job security, for instance, is inconceivable to the general public, let alone the judiciary.

Whether the reader accepts the conclusion that the judiciary is committed to what it sees as individualism and opposed to what it recognizes as collective power one assertion is, it is submitted, incontestable. In a politically fraught area such as labour law statutory interpretation is only superficially about the meaning of words. Words are a malleable commodity in the hands of the judicial strategist. What appears as surprising is the remarkable consistency of that strategy which makes the political intention of the legislature appear unpredictably variable. If that is accepted but the conclusion as to what that strategy is which has been developed in this chapter is doubted, the challenge is clear. Let it be shown that a significantly different strategy is more likely on the evidence.

Notes

*   This chapter was written before the Employment Rights Act 1996 was enacted. This is a consolidation measure: it does not alter the law analysed in this chapter, much of which is now in the 1996 Act but with different section numbers.

1   Wedderburn, *Industrial Relations and the Courts* (1980) 9 ILJ 65 at 78.
2   Davies and Freedland, *Labour Legislation and Public Policy* (OUP, 1995), Ch. 4.
3   Cmnd 3888/1969.
4   Cmnd 3623/1968.
5   [1952] Ch. 646.
6   Trade Disputes Act, 1906, section 3.
7   (1853) 2 E&B 216.
8   [1910] AC 495.
9   See: Wedderburn, *Industrial Relations and Courts* (1980) 9 ILJ 65.
10 [1898] AC 1.
11 [1905] AC 239.
12 [1964] AC 1129.
13 Paragraph 937.
14 [1968] 2 QB at 730.
15 [1977] ICR 61.
16 See, for example, *Secretary of State for Employment v ASLEF (No. 2)* [1972] 2 QB 455; *Faust v Power Packing Casemakers Limited* [1983] IRLR 117.
17 *Brimelow v Casson* [1924] 1 Ch. 302.
18 *Torquay Hotels Company Limited v Cousins* [1969] 2 Ch. 106; confirmed in *Merkur Island Shipping Corporation v Laughton* [1983] ICR 490, which went so far as to hold that the unlawful act could be an inducement to breach of contract by employees other than those employed by one of the parties to the dispute.
19 [1965] AC 269.
20 [1966] 1 All ER 1013.
21 *The Discipline of the Law* (1979) pages 178–9.
22 [1964] AC 1129.
23 See, Wedderburn (1961) 24 MLR 572; (1962) 25 MLR 513.
24 [1987] IRLR 3.
25 [1982] IRLR 102.
26 [1979] ICR 867 at 886.
27 [1980] AC 672 at 695.
28 [1980] ICR 161 at 177.
29 Employment Act 1982 Section 15.
30 [1968] 2 QB 710.
31 [1964] AC 1129.
32 [1942] AC 435; but see *Huntley v Thornton* [1957] 1 WLR 321.
33 Trade Union and Labour Relations (Consolidation) Act 1992 Section 219 (1) (b).
34 It is possible that weaknesses were seen in it as a weapon following the decision in *Morgan v Fry* [1968] QB 710.

35   Section 29.
36   Employment Act 1982 Section 18. See now Trade Union and Labour Relations (Consolidation) Act 1992 Section 244. '... a "trade dispute" means a dispute between workers and their employer which relates wholly or mainly to one or more of the following –

   (a)   terms and conditions of employment, or the physical conditions in which any workers are required to work;
   (b)   engagement or non-engagement, or termination or suspension of employment or the duties of employment of one or more workers;
   (c)   allocation of work or the duties of employment between workers or groups of workers;
   (d)   matters of discipline;
   (e)   a worker's membership or non-membership of a trade union;
   (f)   facilities for officials of trade unions; and
   (g)   machinery for negotiation or consultation, and other procedures, relating to any of the above matters, including recognition by employers or employers' associations of the right of a trade union to represent workers in such negotiation or consultation in the carrying out of such procedures.'

37   *MWL v Woods* [1979] IRLR 478.
38   *BDC v Hearn* [1977] IRLR 269; *MWL v N Woods, supra.*
39   [1980] ICR 42.
40   Page 56.
41   For other cases in the series see particularly *NWL v Woods, supra; Duport Steels Limited v Sirs, supra.* See also [1980] 9 ILJ 65. Griffiths, *The Politics of the Judiciary* (3rd ed. 1985) at page 206 states that the difference between the majority view of the House of Lords and the view of the Court of Appeal only represented 'a clear difference of tactics'. The Employment Act 1980 was already before Parliament when the House of Lords gave its decision in *Express Newspapers.*
42   See *Associated British Ports v TGWU* [1989] IRLR 305.
43   [1983] All ER 189.
44   [1987] 2 All ER 1016.
45   See for example, *Taylor v NUM (Derbyshire Area) (No. 1)* and *Taylor v NUM (Yorkshire Area)* [1985] IRLR 440 and 445.
46   [1985] IRLR 136.
47   [1982] IRLR 200, approved by Lord Goff in *Dimskal Shipping Company SA v ITWF* [1992] IRLR 78.
48   [1982] ICR 114.
49   [1981] ICR 690.
50   [1984] Ch. 27; [1984] ICR 74.
51   Davies and Freedland, *Labour and the Law* (3rd ed. 1983) at page 317.
52   [1984] IRLR 291 (Ch. D.); [1989] IRLR 305 (CA); [1989] IRLR 399 (HL).
53   [1984] 1 WLR 427; 1984 IRLR 161.
54   This has been described as a policy of no victimization; see, S.D. Anderman, *The Status Quo Issue and Industrial Dispute Procedures* (1974) 3 ILJ 131.
55   Employment Act 1982 Section 9. See now Trade Union and Labour Relations (Consolidation) Act 1992 Section 238.
56   Trade Union and Labour Relations (Consolidation) Act 1992 Section 237.
57   [1978] IRLR 82.
58   [1982] IRLR 377.

59   Phillips J., more judiciously, in *Laffin and Callaghan v Fashion Industries (Hartlepool) Limited* [1978] IRLR 448, said, 'to give carte blanche to the loyalty of those who did work is likely to cause indignation among those who, out of a corresponding loyalty to their fellow workmen, did not stay loyal to the management.'

60   [1983] IRLR 117.

61   Section 238 (2) (a) of the 1992 Act.

62   [1989] IRLR 254.

63   The section provides as follows:

'An employee has the right not to have action short of dismissal taken against him as an individual by his employer for the purpose of –

(a)   preventing him or deterring him for being or seeking to become a member of an independent trade union, or penalising him for doing so,

(b)   preventing or deterring him from taking part in the activities of an independent trade union at an appropriate time, or penalising him for doing so.'

64   Section 23 (1).

65   There is a parallel division dealing with dismissal in the 1978 Act Section 58 and in the 1992 Act Section 152 which is worded slightly differently.

66   [1974] IRLR 22.

67   [1987] IRLR 80.

68   [1993] IRLR 336 (CA); [1995] IRLR 258 (HL).

69   See Lord Goff in *James v Eastleigh Borough Council* [1990] IRLR 288.

70   Trade Union Reform and Employment Rights Act 1993, section 13, inserting into the Trade Union and Labour Relations (Consolidation) Act 1992, section 148 (3), an amendment.

71   Sections 11 to 16. See, Simpson, *Judicial Control of ACAS* (1979) 9 ILJ 69.

72   Section 18.

73   *UKAPE v ACAS* [1980] 1 All ER 612.

74   C. Crouch, 'Changing Perceptions of a Public Interest' in *Labour and the Community* (ed. Wedderburn and Murphy, 1982).

75   *Hindle v Percival Boats Ltd* [1969] 1 WLR 174.

76   *Johnson v Nottinghamshire Combined Police Authority* [1974] ICR 170 at 176.

77   [1982] IRLR 177.

78   See, Honeyball, 'Employment Law and the Primacy of Contract' (1989) 18 ILJ 97.

79   See for example, Rideout, 'Implied Terms in the Employment Relationship' in *Exploring the Boundaries of Contract* (ed. Halson, 1995). Compare: *White v Reflecting Roadstuds Ltd* [1991] IRLR 331; *Courtaulds v Sibson* [1988] IRLR 305; *Reid v Rush and Tompkins* [1989] IRLR 265; with *Prestwick Circuits Ltd v McAndrew* [1991] IRLR 191; *United Bank Ltd v Akhtar* [1989] IRLR 597; *Laughton v Bapp* [1986] IRLR 245.

80   O. Kahn-Freund, 'Legal Framework' in A. Flanders and H.A. Clegg (eds.), *The System of Industrial Relations in Great Britain* at p. 47.

81   *The Worker and the Law* (3rd ed.) (Penguin).

82   Fryer, 'The Myths of the Redundancy Payments Act' (1973) 2 ILJ 1; Grunfeld, *Law of Redundancy* (3rd ed.) pp. 2–3.

83   See: Trade Union and Labour Relations (Consolidation) Act 1992 s. 188.

84   Employment Protection (Consolidation) Act 1978 s. 81 (2).

85   *Moon v Homeworthy Furniture (Northern) Ltd* [1977] ICR 177.

86   *R.H. McCulloch Ltd. v Moore* [1968] 1 QB 360; *O'Brien v Associated Firm Alarms*

Ltd [1968] 1 WLR 1916; *Stevenson v Teesside Bridge and Engineering Ltd* [1971] 1 All ER 296; *United Kingdom Atomic Energy Authority v Claydon* [1974] ICR 128.

87   *Supra.*

88   See *United Bank Ltd v Akhtar, supra.*

89   *Supra.*

90   [1994] IRLR 104.

91   For example, *Cowen v Haden Ltd* [1983] ICR 1.

92   For example *European Chefs (Catering) Ltd. v Currell* (1971) ITR 37; *Murphy v Epsom College* [1984] IRLR 271.

93   For example *Nelson v BBC* [1977] ICR 649.

94   *Chapman v Goonvean and Rostowrack China Clay Co.* [1973] ICR 310; *Lesney Products Ltd v Nolan* [1977] ICR 235.

95   For example, *Robinson v British Island Airways* [1978] ICR 304.

96   It never was necessary to do so. It might well have produced less haphazard results if the employee had been permitted to claim whenever the employment relationship terminated by reason of redundancy.

97   HC Deb., Vol 318 columns 1392–1414, May 13, 1971.

98   *Sutcliffe v Hawker Siddely Aviation Ltd* [1973] ICR 560.

99   One wonders what he would make of the judgment of Lord Bridge in *Wilson v Associated Newspapers* [1955] IRLR 258.

100 This line of reasoning would have been closed by the decision of the House of Lords in *Rigby v Ferodo Ltd* [1988] ICR 29.

101 Compare: *The Gaelic Oil Co. Ltd. v Hamilton* [1977] IRLR 27; *Gilbert v I Goldstone Ltd* [1977] ICR 36; *Logabax Ltd v Titherley* [1977] ICR 369; *Turner v London Transport Executive* [1977] ICR 952 per Megaw L.J.; *Scott v Aveling Barford Ltd* [1977] IRLR 419 – all asserting the test of unreasonable conduct – with *Wetherall (Bond St, W1) Ltd v Lynn* [1977] IRLR 333; *Western Excavating (ECC) Ltd. v Sharp* [1978] 1 All ER 713 – ultimately establishing the contractual test.

102 *Walker v Josiah Wedgwood and Sons Ltd* [1978] ICR 744.

103 *Walker v Josiah Wedgwood, supra*; *Graham Oxley Tool Steels Ltd. v Firth* [1980] IRLR 369.

104 *W.E. Cox Toner (International) Ltd v Crook* [1981] ICR 823 – in which a liberal view was taken of the conclusion to be drawn from the fact of the employee remaining at work without protest.

105 *Haseltine Lake and Co. v Dowler* [1981] ICR 222; *Financial Techniques (Planning Service) Ltd. v Hughes* [1981] IRLR 32.

106 One of the earliest examples is *Isle of Wight Tourist Board v Coombes* [1976] IRLR 43 the facts of which are by no means so wide ranging as is usually assumed. By far the most interesting is the decision of Professor B.A. Hepple in *Wood v Freeloader Ltd* [1977] IRLR 455.

107 *Principles of Labour Law* (3rd Ed., 1979) (Sweet and Maxwell) at p. 94.

108 Painter, Holmes and Migdal, *Cases and Materials on Employment Law* (1995, Blackstone Press Ltd.) at p. 327.

109 *Woods v W.M. Car Services (Peterborough) Ltd* [1982] ICR 693.

110 [1981] ICR 666.

4   Interpreting Tax Statutes

Jacqueline Dyson

Introduction

The object of this chapter is to examine recent developments in interpretation of tax statutes by the courts, and to consider future trends in the light of
possible changes in the style of tax legislation. Interpretation of legislation
does not take place in a vacuum; it takes place in the context of the legal
system of which it is a part. The rules of interpretation which have developed in the United Kingdom reflect this, and in considering approaches to
interpretation of tax statutes it is essential to have regard to the style of
drafting of the legislation which is to be interpreted. Drafting and interpretation are mutually dependent.[1]

It is intended to demonstrate that a more purposive approach to interpretation of fiscal legislation is being adopted by the courts. This shows in areas
such as tax avoidance, where the courts have not been deflected by complex
legislation from considering the underlying purpose of the law. The more
purposive approach should, and may encourage legislators to draft less
complex legislation.

Problems with Tax Legislation

Pressures for change in the drafting of tax legislation are mounting. Every
year practitioners complain about the length and complexity of the Finance
Act. This is not new. There is general agreement that something must be
done. Not only are the professionals weighed down, both literally and
metaphorically, but even the Inland Revenue has acknowledged the problem
and is actively considering it.[2]

The fundamental principle is that in order to exact tax from taxpayers
there must be clear authority of Parliament.[3] Statutes and the interpretation
of statutes are therefore essential to the law of taxation. However, to satisfy

all the requirements for a good tax system would probably be unachievable.[4] One requirement is certainty, another is simplicity to aid comprehensibility for the users. This raises the question of who are the users of the tax legislation. Is the legislation addressed to the ordinary taxpayer? The Meade Report[5] focused on the ordinary taxpayer and the need for accountability when it stated:

> In a democratic society one of the most important aspects of a tax system is that the taxing authorities should be accountable to the electorate at large. This can be so only if the tax system is such that the man and woman in the street can comprehend clearly what is the nature of the taxpayers' liability.[6]

However, the UK tax system assumes that there is no need for most ordinary taxpayers, who are employees, to understand the legislation or even the tax system, as the PAYE system is operated by the employer. This will not alter with the change to self-assessment. The reality is that the legislation has been considered as addressing specialist advisers and the Inland Revenue, not taxpayers directly.[7] At present the tax legislation clearly fails to satisfy Meade's ideal of comprehension by the man in the street. This is hardly surprising since this has not been the aim of legislators.

There is no doubt that the length of tax legislation has increased dramatically in recent years. This is fuelling the protests about the legislation thus leading to a serious reappraisal of the drafting of tax legislation. For the first time in 1994 the Finance Bill was printed in two volumes. Beighton highlighted the problem in his recent Hardman Lecture where he acknowledged the position stating: 'In the last five years we have seen over 1,300 pages of primary legislation put on to the Statute Book'.[8]

Complex tax legislation has been with us for a long time. There are many reasons for this. Some are true of all legislation, but many are exclusively related to tax legislation. Complexity may be partly a reflection of the fact that the legislation is being drafted by tax specialists for tax specialists who can be expected to cope with difficult legislation. However the increased complexity leads to an increased compliance burden. Even the Government acknowledges the problem; the Financial Secretary to the Treasury said this year, 'Coming new to tax legislation, I must confess that I was struck by the complexity of some of the legislation and the volume of it.'[9] This problem of incomprehensibility is not unique to the United Kingdom but is also true of other jurisdictions. Prebble in his amusing article 'Why is Tax Law Incomprehensible?' attempts an explanation for this in relation to New Zealand tax legislation which would be equally applicable here.[10]

A general problem in the approach to drafting of fiscal legislation in the United Kingdom is that an attempt is made to deal with all possible contingencies.[11] Amendments are added to sections where a gap is apparent, and as the detail increases the legislation becomes even more dense. This ensures that the legislation becomes more complex. An example of this detailed drafting is the present rules for the taxation of gilts and bonds. A recent press release[12] acknowledges that the rules for the different types of bonds are very complex and long,[13] and that if there is no radical reform there will need to be yet more legislation to deal with new types of bonds. In spite of detailed drafting, some fiscal legislation still lacks clarity, and in some instances there is uncertainty about its application to particular situations. The Inland Revenue publish a variety of information, such as statements of practice and press releases, to deal with some of these uncertainties. They now publish Revenue Interpretations to explain the Revenue view of some uncertain areas of the law and internal manuals. There is also the recent experiment on post-transaction rulings and discussion for the future of a system of pre-transaction rulings.[14]

A fundamental problem is that our income tax system is old and was not designed for the sophisticated financial world in which we live today. In adapting existing legislation to embrace new situations, the style of drafting that is generally used is to graft on to the existing law additional charges instead of reviewing the whole area and making a fresh, coherent charge.[15] Even where a new tax is introduced with a simple concept, such as Capital Transfer Tax, exemptions and reliefs for certain groups of taxpayers are added.[16] This detracts from the initial simplicity. More recently the Finance Acts have become excessively complicated.[17] The result is that fiscal statutes are a mess and lead Gammie to ask 'Legislation for business: is it fit for public consumption?'[18] Tiley concludes that, 'The result might be described as a patchwork were it not for the overtones of antique cosiness that go with that word; it is better described as a shambles.'[19]

The Hansard Commission Report examined the Parliamentary process for the enactment of legislation. It found some general problems and made suggestions for change.[20] One unsurprising judgment was that 'legislative business is often too rushed.'[21] With tax legislation the timetable is imposed by the deadlines leading up to the annual Finance Act. There is a tension between the constraints of a timetable imposed by political and economic considerations and the longer time often required for the enactment of clear legislation.[22] The change in the time of the Budget from the Spring to November has not increased the time for Parliament to consider the Finance Bill.[23] Many suggestions have been made to alleviate the problem but as yet these have not found favour.[24] Rushed legislation is unlikely to be clear and effective.

Increased consultation on legislation has been advocated as one means of improving certainty and clarity. The Hansard Report[25] referred with approval to the consultation which takes place on draft clauses by the Inland Revenue with representatives from industry and commerce. One difficulty which may result from increased consultation is that it may lead to more complicated legislation, as the consultation is with tax specialists representing sophisticated clients.[26] The Government's view of consultation was given by the Financial Secretary to the Treasury who said 'every time we consider any serious change in the tax system, it is taken now as an assumption – not simply a consideration, but an assumption – that virtually any substantial change in the tax system is something that would be better implemented after a period of consultation.'[27]

Effective consultation does not always take place for a number of reasons. Political pressures may mean that the Government is unwilling to consult on proposed legislation. An example of this was the introduction of insurance premium tax where the consultation was done after the Budget. Fiscal legislation would have fewer flaws if, where politically possible, the consultative process included the publication of draft legislation.[28]

In his Hamlyn Lectures given in 1981, Hubert Monroe elegantly summarized the position with regard to tax statutes:

> All then are agreed that tax statutes are too long, too obscure and too complex. All are agreed that they are getting longer, more obscure and more complex. The complexities of our society, inevitable high rates of tax, the importunities of worthy pressure groups, the ingenuity of less worthy groups of tax avoiders, the imperfections, here and there, of our Parliamentary machinery for presenting, reviewing and passing legislation, all these – it is argued – are to be identified as the causes of our discontents.[29]

Since this was written the rates of tax have been reduced but nothing has changed in this description of the tax statutes.

Interpretation of Tax Legislation

It has been observed that the style of legislation evolves in the society of the time, and equally the style of interpretation of that legislation is subject to the influences of the epoch.[30] Detailed rules for interpretation can be found in specialist books such as Maxwell and Bennion;[31] however as Viscount Simonds observed 'Support of the very highest authority can be found for general and apparently irreconcilable propositions'.[32] One problem with fiscal legislation is that the courts are often concerned with interpretation of consolidating acts.[33] It is proposed here, however, to examine the factors influencing recent trends in interpretation in the area of taxation. There have been three major developments: first, the change in the judicial approach to tax avoidance, second the effect of the decision of the House of Lords in *Pepper v Hart*,[34] and third the increasing influence on our courts of European legislation and decisions of the European Court.

Before turning to the three developments, it is useful to summarize briefly the general position on interpretation. The often quoted decision of Lord Cairns in *Partington v A.G.*[35] stated the principle of literal construction in a case about probate duty. Lord Cairns said:

> If the person sought to be taxed comes within the letter of the law he must be taxed, however great the hardship may appear to the judicial mind to be. On the other hand, if the Crown, seeking to recover the tax, cannot bring the subject within the letter of the law, the subject is free, however apparently within the spirit of the law the case might otherwise appear to be. In other words, if there be admissible in any statute, what is called an equitable construction, certainly such a construction is not admissible in a taxing statute, where you can simply adhere to the words of the statute.

This approach was also taken in the celebrated case of *Tennant v Smith*,[36] where Lord Halsbury emphasized the provisions of the Act as expressed and rejected the consideration of purpose.

It was in an article by Willis[37] that the principles of interpretation were solidified into the three rules, known as the literal, golden and mischief rules. Although it is clear that these are not immutable rules and are better described as approaches to statutory interpretation, they are often still referred to as rules. It is more appropriate and helpful to think in terms of approaches to interpretation.[38] Ward also considers that 'it is meaningful to talk of distinctive interpretive "approaches".[39]

The literal approach is grammatical, but it is also described as a 'strict approach', that is keeping to the actual words of the statute. Is the approach to statutory interpretation different in statutes dealing with taxation from other areas of the law? It has been suggested that fiscal legislation should be more strictly interpreted because it is penal, and analogous to the criminal law. In *Cross on Statutory Interpretation*, there is a discrete section on the presumption against unclear changes in the law and revenue statutes.[40] It is obviously correct that there must be clear authority to charge taxpayers. This does not, however, automatically lead to a stricter approach generally to the interpretation of fiscal legislation. Mr Justice Vinelott explored this question and concluded 'that there are no special principles of construction applicable only to fiscal legislation'.[41] Ward also supports this view 'that no special considerations apply to tax statute in the United Kingdom context, so far as the *general* approach to interpretation is concerned'.[42]

The so called 'golden rule' has traditionally been applied to legislation in order to deal with the situation where following a literal approach would produce absurdity, as, for example, in *O'Rourke v Binks*.[43] The definition of absurdity is difficult.[44] As Popkin writes: 'although the concept of absurdity which can be used to trump a clear text can be stretched, it is not very broad'. He contrasts this with the position in the US where it is routine for judges to consider statutory purpose.[45] The golden rule has been described by Zander 'as an unpredictable safety valve to permit the courts to escape from some of the more unpalatable effects of the literal rule'.[46] There are alternative approaches for the courts in this situation: either to follow what Bennion calls a 'strained construction'[47] of the actual words used by Parliament, thus adhering to the literal approach or to look to the presumed intention of Parliament. The decision in *Pepper v Hart*[48] now allows reference to parliamentary material where there is found to be absurdity. Lord Browne-Wilkinson held that parliamentary material should be permitted as an aid to the construction of legislation which is ambiguous or obscure or the literal meaning leads to an absurdity. Reference on the grounds of ambiguity or obscurity has been the usual route.

The starting point today for statutory construction in tax cases is the literal approach. As Tiley puts it 'one should assume that the courts will at least begin with a presumption in favour of a strict or literal interpretation'.[49] Mr Justice Vinelott in an article in 1982[50] acknowledged that the courts do not confine themselves to a rigid literal approach:

> If what is meant by the literalist approach is that if the words of a statute are clear and the results are not blatantly at odds with the scheme to be inferred from the legislation as a whole and do not lead to a blatantly capricious or arbitrary result the task of the judge is to give effect to those words, then the literalist approach as I see it clearly states the proper approach to statutory interpretation. By contrast *Luke v IRC*[51] shows that if the words of a particular provision literally construed lead to a result which is unjust to the taxpayer or at odds with the scope of the scheme of taxation to be inferred from the legislation as a whole, then the courts can mould even clear language of the particular provision to produce a more harmonious and fair result. If all that is meant by the purposivist approach is that the courts can in such circumstances depart from literal interpretation then the purposivist case can also be conceded.[52]

In *Luke v IRC*,[53] which was a case about the interpretation of the legislation charging benefits in kind, it was presumed that Parliament could not have intended to enact legislation that would produce an unreasonable result. The House of Lords found a possible interpretation which produced a reasonable result and applied it in deciding the case. It is interesting to note that it was also interpretation of legislation charging benefits in kind and the expense incurred which gave rise to the decision in *Pepper v Hart*.

A recent example of the current approach to interpretation of fiscal legislation is to be found in the case of *Sutherland v Gustar*.[54] Here the Court of Appeal was faced with construing the provisions of section 31 of the Taxes Management Act 1970 for partners where there was disagreement among the partners and they did not want to act together in an appeal. The statutory scheme did not provide for this situation, as section 31 merely provides that 'an appeal may be brought against an assessment to tax'. The court refused to adopt a literal approach but relied on the presumed intention of Parliament. Sir Donald Nicholls, Vice-Chancellor explained the approach in this way:

> In these circumstances it would be easy to retreat into adopting a literal approach to the construction of the statutory provisions, while criticising the much-maligned parliamentary draftsmen for compelling the court to reach an unsatisfactory result, and adding as a rider an expression of pious hope that Parliament will take an early opportunity to reconsider the matter.
>
> We do not think that is the right approach. Legislation is to be interpreted so as to give effect to Parliament's presumed intention, so long as this is clear, provided always the language of the statute fairly admits of the interpretation in question.

It is apparent from the above that the courts have become more flexible in their approach to statutory interpretation. They still start with a literal approach, but where this fails to provide an answer or produces an unreasonable result, the courts invoke the presumed intention of Parliament. Lord Oliver recognized the danger for judges 'of attributing legislative intention too readily simply because we think that we, the judges, had we been the legislators, would have found such an intention sensible or morally or politically desirable'.[55]

With the trend to a more purposive approach there have been the three specific developments referred to earlier.

Tax Avoidance

The first of these is the dramatic change in the approach of the courts to tax avoidance. Unlike countries such as Australia and New Zealand, the United Kingdom has not had general anti-avoidance legislation.[56] Traditionally the approach has been like a game with tax avoiders, on one side, identifying a loophole in the legislation and then exploiting it in a scheme to avoid tax. The response of the other side has been very specific, hole-plugging legislation designed to counter the scheme, but often bringing within its ambit other transactions. Before the landmark decision in *IRC v Ramsay*,[57] such legislation was given a literal interpretation.

The techniques of the tax avoidance industry and particularly the marketing of off-the-peg schemes led to a change in attitude by the courts to tax avoidance. Although in *Ramsay* it was argued for the taxpayer that a general anti-avoidance attack on schemes was a matter for Parliament, the House of Lords based the change of approach on the interpretation of taxing statutes. Popkin describes this area of judicial creativity as 'one battleground on which the dispute between literalism and statutory purpose has been fought in England'.[58]

In *Ramsay* self-cancelling schemes designed to avoid capital gains tax were defeated by taking a more general purposive interpretation rather than the literal interpretation which had previously prevailed. Lord Wilberforce restated what he described as a familiar principle:

> A subject is only to be taxed on clear words, not on 'intendment' or on the 'equity' of an Act. Any taxing Act of Parliament is to be construed in accordance with this principle. What are 'clear words' is to be ascertained on normal principles; these do not confine the courts to literal interpretation. There may, indeed should, be considered the context and scheme of the relevant Act as a whole, and its purpose may, indeed should be regarded.

Lord Wilberforce claimed not to be introducing a new principle but only a new approach. However it clearly was a new principle and has been referred to in subsequent judgments by, for example, Lord Brightman in *Furniss v Dawson*[59] and Lord Browne-Wilkinson in *Fitzwilliam v IRC*,[60] as 'the Ramsay principle'. The change was for the court in tax avoidance cases to look at the scheme as a whole and to consider the purpose of the steps taken. It was the extension of the *Ramsay* principle in *Furniss v Dawson* to schemes which were not self-cancelling which caused consternation in the tax world. Although perhaps underlying the decision was the implication that the House of Lords was construing the statute, there is no explicit reference to statutory construction in any of the judgments. The focus of the judgments is the attempt to identify the conditions for the *Ramsay* principle to apply. It is only in later decisions of the House of Lords that the emphasis on construction of statutory provisions is to the fore.

The case of *Furniss v Dawson* marked the high point of judicial antipathy to tax avoidance. Succeeding cases provide limits on the new principle, and the tensions involved in finding those limits are demonstrated by the fact that some of the post *Dawson* decisions are by majority unlike *Ramsay*, *Burmah*[61] and *Dawson*. The decision in *Craven v White*[62] is one where all members of the House of Lords emphasize that they are engaged in statutory construction although there is a fundamental division between them in their conclusions on the facts. Lord Goff, one of the minority, rejects the suggestion that the principle is a moral one but recognizes the *Ramsay* principle as one of statutory construction. He elaborates this in the following words:

> In each case, your Lordships' House has been seeking to ascertain the true intention of Parliament when it has applied the words of the statute to the facts of the case before it; and in so far as your Lordships have been attempting, in any particular case, a statement of principle, that statement of principle has been an attempt to formulate the parliamentary intention with an eye to the facts of that particular case.[63]

This is a clear statement of a purposive approach to statutory interpretation in the tax avoidance area.

Although there has been some retrenchment in the tax avoidance cases since *Furniss v Dawson*,[64] the move away from a literal interpretation to a more purposive interpretation in this area has been confirmed.

Pepper v Hart

The second major change in the approach to statutory interpretation was the landmark decision in *Pepper v Hart*.[65] Again the effect of the decision was a shift from a strict, literal approach to a more purposive approach. Prior to *Pepper v Hart*, where there was ambiguity in fiscal legislation, this was interpreted in favour of the taxpayer on the basis that the subject should only be taxed by clear words. Indeed this was the conclusion of the Lord Chancellor in *Pepper v Hart* itself.[66]

The decision, by a majority of a House of Lords of six to one, was that in limited circumstances reference to parliamentary materials is permissible. Those circumstances were set out in the leading judgment of Lord Browne-Wilkinson that reference to parliamentary material should be permitted as an aid to the construction of legislation which is ambiguous or obscure or the literal meaning of which leads to an absurdity. The statement in parliament which is relied on has to be clear[67] and to have been made by the minister or other promoter of the Bill. This decision changed hundreds of years of judicial self-imposed restraint in referring to parliamentary material.

The facts of *Pepper v Hart* were simple. Schoolmasters were assessed to tax on the benefit in kind received as a result of having their sons educated at the school for concessionary fees. The question of interpretation for the courts was what was the taxable amount of this benefit. The legislation provided that it 'is an amount equal to the cost of the benefit', and further that 'the cost of a benefit is the amount of any expense incurred in or in connection with its provision, including a proper proportion of any expense relating partly to the benefit and partly to other matters'.[68] Reference to *Hansard* showed that it was clear that the Financial Secretary intended the cost in this situation to be the marginal cost rather than the average cost for which the Revenue had argued.[69] This was obviously an important decision on the taxation of in-house benefits in kind, but the decision permitting reference to parliamentary material was of immense significance for the interpretation of all legislation.

One of the main concerns of the judges in reaching the decision in *Pepper v Hart* was the practical difficulty of accessibility to parliamentary material and the added expense of litigation. This was the stated reason for the dissent of the Lord Chancellor. The difficulties of researching *Hansard* have been written about.[70] *Hansard* is also so expensive that as currently priced it cannot be widely available.[71] However in these times of technological advances, it seems that there is a demand for *Hansard* to be available more widely. It should become possible to achieve this without undue expense, perhaps through electronic information networks.

The question of which parliamentary materials may be consulted was not dealt with in the decision – for example, the position of press releases as discussed in Whiteman.[72] If these do have ministerial approval but are not specifically referred to in answer to a question, are they admissible parliamentary material? This is of importance for the annual Budget press releases and it is difficult to see why they should not be admissible. The Chancellor's Budget statement was referred to in *Walters v Tickner*.[73] Normally the press releases will explain the intention behind the legislation. This raises the constitutional problem that, in reality, the judges are not seeking the intention of Parliament but the intention of the Inland Revenue or Customs and Excise. As Williams wrote in 1978 'Finance Bills are creatures of the Treasury and Revenue advisers'.[74]

The decision in *Pepper v Hart* permitted reference to parliamentary material but only in limited circumstances. It appears from subsequent cases that those limits are not being observed in practice. One of the reasons for this is that there was no definition in the case of the meaning of ambiguity, obscurity or absurdity. In many cases concerning interpretation of a statute, it will at least be arguable that there is some ambiguity or obscurity. Even where it is held that these conditions are not satisfied judges are using *Pepper v Hart* to confirm their interpretation of the legislation. A recent example of this is to be found in decision of the Court of Appeal in *Petch v Gurney*.[75] Here Millett L.J. held it was not appropriate to invoke the principle in *Pepper v Hart* for the absence of any power to extend the time limit laid down by section 56(4) Taxes Management Act 1970 is too plain for argument. But as it happens examination of the extract from *Hansard* confirms the impression which is conveyed by the words quoted.

Even where the conditions for reference to parliamentary materials are satisfied, often nothing useful will be found to assist in interpretation. This may be for two reasons. First there may have been no discussion of the relevant section, and second even where there was debate this may not elucidate the point of difficulty.[76] Williams in his article on the Finance Act gives the interesting statistic that of the 211 clauses in the first print 130 were not discussed at all.[77] Lord Browne-Wilkinson's prediction about the helpfulness of reference to *Hansard* is being confirmed. 'In many, I suspect most, cases references to Parliamentary materials will not throw any light on the matter. But in a few cases it may emerge that the very question was considered by Parliament in passing the legislation.'[78]

There is a danger which is discussed by Miers, of a change in the nature of parliamentary debate.[79] Ministers will have the decision in *Pepper* in mind in answering questions, and will either be very cautious in keeping to their brief, or use the opportunity to make a statement elaborating government intention anticipating that this may be referred to in the courts at a later stage. It is suggested by Jenkins that this may lead to draftsmen playing a more active role in vetting briefings for ministers.[80]

All these fears are about practical matters in the operation of the non exclusionary rule and observation over time will show whether the fears are justified. Lord Browne-Wilkinson is alert to these concerns, but observes in his speech that 'experience in Commonwealth countries which have abandoned the rule does not suggest that the drawbacks are substantial, provided that the courts keeps a tight control on the circumstances in which reference to parliamentary material are allowed.'[81]

The House of Lords acknowledges that the courts now adopt a purposive approach. Lord Griffiths states that

> The days have long passed when the courts adopted a strict constructionalist view of interpretation which required them to adopt the literal meaning of the language. The courts now adopt a purposive approach which seeks to give effect to the true purpose of legislation and are prepared to look at much extraneous material that bears on the background against which the legislation was enacted.[82]

And Lord Browne-Wilkinson similarly

> Given the purposive approach to construction now adopted by the courts in order to give effect to the true intentions of the legislature, the fine distinctions

between looking for the mischief and looking for the intention in using words to provide the remedy are technical and inappropriate.[83]

The decision in *Pepper v Hart*, permitting reference to parliamentary materials to ascertain the intention of Parliament, is itself another step towards giving a greater emphasis to a purposive approach to interpretation.[84]

The European Influence

The third development in statutory interpretation is the increasing importance of European legislation. Membership of the European Union has led to the United Kingdom courts having to interpret Community law. The result is that the courts are gaining familiarity both with a different style of legislation and different techniques of interpretation.[85] The main difference in the legislation is that the European style is to lay down general principles rather than specific, detailed legislation favoured in the UK. Millett identifies four characteristics of European community legislation which mould it.[86] These are that there is a grand design for integration; the attempt to achieve uniformity with 15 member states; the fact of nine Community languages[87] which results in the literal meaning of legislation not being conclusive as to meaning; and the existence of preambles to Community legislation giving reasons for the provisions. These characteristics lead to the dominance in interpretation of contextual and teleological approaches unlike the predominance of the literal approach in the UK.

There are three methods of interpretation used in the Court of Justice: the literal, schematic and teleological.[88] The schematic, or contextual, method takes into account the grand design of Community law, and so it is necessary to understand other provisions of Community law. The teleological focuses on the purpose or object of the legislation. This is possible and appropriate for Community legislation where objectives are given and there are recitals at the beginning of legislation which state reasons for adopting the provision. The result of this approach is that, unlike in the UK, the teleological interpretation can override a clear literal meaning. It can also be used to fill gaps in legislation[89] in contrast to the House of Lords which is reluctant to appear to legislate.[90]

An example of this approach to interpretation by the Court of Justice is to be found in the case of *Apple and Pear Council v Customs and Excise*.[91] Here the question was whether the exercise by the Council of its functions constituted a supply of services effected for consideration within the meaning of Art 2(1) of EC Council Directive 77/388 in the harmonization of the laws of member states relating to turnover taxes: common system of value added tax: uniform basis of assessment. The problem was that the Second

Directive which had used the phrase 'against payment' was replaced by the Sixth Directive which changed the phrase to 'for consideration'. The Court of Justice looked at the legislative objective of the Directives, and so was not bound by the difference in the precise words, and thus was able to take into account the judgments of the Court on the Second Directive.

> The object of both directives was to harmonise the laws of member states relating to turnover taxes, to establish a common system and a uniform basis of assessment. Each of the language versions must have been intended to have the same meaning and to achieve the same object. It would, therefore be wrong to construe the phrase 'supply ... effected for consideration' in the light of the technical meaning of the words in English domestic law, as it would equally be wrong to construe the other language texts by reference to their technical meaning in the appropriate domestic law. To give such technical meanings to the words would be capable of producing, if not likely to produce, diversity rather than harmonisation. The words must thus be construed in their community law context as a community law phrase, regard being had to the different language versions.[92]

The decision was that the exercise of the Council's functions did not constitute a supply of services effected for consideration.

In the European Union the governing consideration is the general purpose of the law, which is very different from the UK approach. Brown and Kennedy conclude in their chapter on Methods of Interpretation that 'The earlier reliance on literal interpretation has given place increasingly to the contextual and teleological approaches, approaches which befit a jurisdiction charged with a quasi-constitutional function as the guardian of the grand objectives laid down in the Treaties.'[93] In the UK the most obvious area of tax in which the European influence has been manifest so far is Value Added Tax.[94] VAT is a form of tax required by the European Community, and the provisions of UK VAT legislation must conform with the EC Council Directive 77/388, the Sixth Directive. The principle is stated in the speech of Lord Keith in *Webb v. EMO Air Cargo (UK) Ltd*[95]

> it is for a United Kingdom court to construe domestic legislation in any field covered by a Community directive so as to accord with the interpretation of the directive as laid down by the European Court, if that can be done without distorting the meaning of the domestic legislation.' A recent example of this is to be found in the case of *Customs and Excise Commrs v. British Telecom plc.*[96] Here the court was interpreting UK VAT Regulations and did so in conformity with the Sixth Directive. The influence of European legislation with its broad principles, together with European methods of interpretation, is likely to increase in the UK courts.[97]

The Way Forward

Fundamental reforms to simplify tax law itself would mean less legislation and greater comprehensibility.[98] Many of the current complications in income tax law arise because of the age of the basic structure of the law. Prebble suggests that the main problem areas are geography, time and the distinction between income and capital.[99] Legislation directed at avoidance schemes which take advantage of gaps has been shown to be particularly detailed and complex. In examining the development of tax legislation, Gammie observes 'However, tax avoidance can be one of the best guides to the deficiencies inherent in the tax system because those who seek to avoid tax are by definition playing on the system's weaknesses.'[100]

The Chairman of the Law Commission recently described its mission as being 'to make law simpler, fairer and cheaper to use'.[101] The Law Commission has not, however, tackled fiscal legislation in its programme.

The immediate way forward, however, lies with the recommendations of two separate bodies which have examined and reported on the simplification of fiscal legislation. The Tax Law Review Committee, set up in November 1994 by the Institute of Fiscal Studies, examined tax legislation as its first project. The Committee produced an interim report in November 1995 and a final report in June 1996. Their main recommendations were that tax legislation should be drafted in plain language, that explanatory memoranda would assist in interpretation, and that there should be a pilot study on rewriting tax legislation.

The second body which has examined simplification of tax legislation is the Inland Revenue itself. Section 160 Finance Act 1995 required the Inland Revenue to prepare a report on tax simplification by December 1995. This report, entitled 'The Path to Tax Simplification', considered as possible solutions: policy reform, reform of the Finance Bill procedure, and improving the language and organization of existing law.[102] The third of these was recommended as the most likely to yield improvements and has been followed by a consultative document, 'Tax Law Rewrite – The Way Forward', with detailed suggestions for rewriting existing tax legislation over five years.[103]

The investigations of both these bodies took into account similar work being done overseas, particularly in New Zealand[104] and in Australia. The Australian Tax Law Improvement Project has as its principal objects to create tax legislation with 'a clear, easy to follow structure' and to 'use plain concise English'.[105] Some pilot legislation in simple form has been enacted.[106] There are already comments on the difficulties involved and criticisms of the new approach to drafting.[107]

Quite apart from any simplification of the language used by the legislators, general principles drafting could be used so that the courts could go further than they have in adopting a purposive method of construing Finance Acts. This suggestion is at the core of Beighton's argument in his 1994 Hardman Lecture, and in his recent comments on the two reports on tax simplification in the *British Tax Review*.[108] Although he is expressing a personal view, it is that of an insider as he was Deputy Chairman of the Board of Inland Revenue. It is also the theme of Avery Jones' article entitled 'Tax law: rules or principles?'[109]

In applying a more purposive interpretation, the courts will need assistance to ascertain the intention of Parliament. The Hansard Report recommended that notes on sections, including Schedules, explaining the purpose and intended effect of each section, should be prepared by Government departments with the assistance of Parliamentary Counsel and approved by ministers.[110] These explanatory notes, which presently accompany the Finance Bills, could be published with the Finance Acts, and the courts could refer to them as an aid to their understanding. The words of the Act would still prevail unless they do not provide an answer. This use of explanatory memoranda was recommended by the Tax Law Review Committee and appears to be acceptable to the government.[111] For Finance Acts, the detailed notes on sections would be helpful to the courts in explaining the purpose of the legislation.[112] In addition to explanatory notes, worked examples could be included for some sections to assist the courts. The result would be a commentary making the purpose clear. The courts could then have regard to the true intention of Parliament (in reality the minister) rather than being tied to the words of the statute. This would represent a considerable improvement in the interpretation of tax statutes.

This survey of the approach of the legislators and the courts to fiscal legislation shows that, whilst the courts have an important role to play in cutting through the complexities and obscurities of the draftsman's language, the problem calls for more radical treatment than is, or is likely to be, capable of being administered by the judges alone. Recent proposals for rewriting tax legislation will provide improvements for the interpretation of tax statutes, but the pressure for more fundamental change remains.

Notes

1 Bell and Engle, *Cross on Statutory Interpretation* (3rd ed. 1995).
2 IR Press Release, 16 Feb. 1995.
3 Bill of Rights 1689, Article 4.
4 Adam Smith, *The Wealth of Nations*, Book V 1776; Meade, *The Structure and Reform of Direct Taxation* (1978 Institute of Fiscal Studies).
5 Ibid.
6 Ibid. at p. 18.

7   MacCormick and Summers, *Interpreting Statutes* (1991, Dartmouth), at p. 394.
8   1995 *BTR* 33. See also the IFS 1994 Annual Report which refers to the longest Finance Bills in history, 1993 312 pages, 1994 463 pages and 1995 375 pages.
9   IR Press Release Feb. 1995, Sir George Young. See also section 160 Finance Act 1995 discussed at p. 25.
10   1994 *BTR* 380, 'Why is Tax Law Incomprehensible?'
11   The Report of the Hansard Society Commission on the Legislative Process, 1992 at para. 234.
12   IR Press Release 25 May 1995, and see IR Press Release 10 July 1995. For detailed comment see 1995 *BTR* 511, Hale, 'The Taxation of Gilts and Bonds'.
13   Over 100 pages of legislation.
14   IR Interpretations from November 1991; IR Consultative Document, Post-Transaction Rulings 1994; IR Press Release 17 Nov 1994; Sandler, *A Request for Rulings*, Institute of Tax 1994.
15   For example, the taxation of fringe benefits.
16   For example, agricultural property, section 115 IHTA 1984.
17   For example, Williams, 'The Finance Act 1993: Incredible drafting extraordinary prose', 1993 *BTR* 483.
18   15 Fiscal Studies 127.
19   Butterworths UK Tax Guide, 1:29.
20   The Report of the Hansard Society Commission on the Legislative Process, 1992 Chapter 5 Parliamentary Processes.
21   Ibid., at para. 316.
22   See Recommendations on the Development of Tax Legislation, The Special Committee of Tax Law Consultative Bodies, 1993.
23   Gammie, 'Budgetary Reform: The Impact of a December Budget on the Finance Bill and the Development of Tax Legislation', *Fiscal Studies* (1993) vol. 14, 95.
24   Howe, 1977 *BTR* 97; Gammie, ibid.
25   Ibid. at paras 73, 108 and 139.
26   'Pruning the Triffid', Ernst & Young, 1994.
27   Stephen Dorrell, 'Budgetary Reform', *Fiscal Studies* (1993) vol. 14, 89 at 94.
28   Recommendations on the Development of Tax Legislation, 1993, The Special Committee of Tax Law Consultative Bodies.
29   Monroe, *Intolerable Inquisition? Reflections on the Law of Tax*, Hamlyn, 1981, at p. 35.
30   Bell and Engle, *Cross on Statutory Interpretation* (3rd ed., 1995).
31   *Maxwell on Interpretation of Statutes* (12th ed., 1969); Bennion, *Statutory Interpretation* (2nd ed., 1992).
32   In *A-G v Prince Ernest Augustus of Hanover* [1957] AC 436 referred to in Butterworths UK Tax Guide 1:30.
33   See Bramwell, 'Interpreting Consolidation Acts: the Influence of History', 1992 *BTR* 69 and Ghosh, 'The Construction of Fiscal Legislation', 1994 *BTR* 126.
34   [1993] AC 593.
35   (1869) LR 4 E&I App HL 100.
36   [1892] AC 150 at 154.
37   Willis, 'Statutory Interpretation in a Nutshell', 16 *Can. Bar Rev.* 1, 1938.
38   Law Commission Report, The Interpretation of Statutes (1969).
39   Ward, 'A Comparative Study of the Interpretation of Tax Statute in the UK and Ireland', 1994 BTR 42 at 44.
40   Bell and Engle, *Cross on Statutory Interpretation* (3rd ed., 1995) p. 180.

41   'Interpretation of Fiscal Statutes', 1982 *Stat. LR* 78.
42   Ward, 'Interpretation of Tax Statute in UK and Ireland', 1994 *BTR* 42 at 43.
43   1992 STC 703. An example of the literal application is described by Scott L.J. as an absurd anomaly, at 708. See discussion of this in Ghosh, 'The Construction of Fiscal Legislation', 1994 *BTR* 126.
44   See discussion in Ward, 1994 *BTR* 42 at 48.
45   Popkin, 'Judicial Anti-Avoidance Doctrine in England', 1991 *BTR* 283 at 287.
46   Zander, *The Law Making Process* (4th ed., 1994), p. 130.
47   Bennion, *Statutory Interpretation* (2nd ed., 1992), at p. 333.
48   [1993] 1 All ER 42.
49   Butterworths UK Tax Guide 1994–95 at 1:30.
50   'Interpretation of Fiscal Statutes', 1982 *Stat LR* 78.
51   [1963] AC 557; [1963] 1 All ER 655.
52   At 85.
53   Ibid.
54   [1994] 4 All ER 1.
55   1992 14 *Statute LR* 1, 'A Judicial View of Modern Legislation'.
56   1994 *BTR* 647, Masters, 'Is there a need for general anti-avoidance legislation in the UK?'
57   [1981] 1 All ER 865.
58   Popkin, 'Judicial Anti-Avoidance Doctrine in England: A United States Perspective', 1991 BTR 283.
59   [1984] 1 All ER 530.
60   [1993] 3 All ER 184.
61   *IRC v Burmah Oil Co.* [1982] STC.
62   [1988] 3 All ER 495.
63   At p. 531 c and j.
64   For example, *Fitzwilliam v IRC* [1993] 3 All ER 184.
65   [1993] 1 All ER 42.
66   At p. 47a.
67   Bates, 'Parliamentary Material and Statutory Construction: Aspects of the Practical Approach of *Pepper v Hart*', 1993 14 *Stat. LR* 46. Bates says that the requirement to be clear should go to weight, not admissibility.
68   Now sections 156(1) & (2) TA 1988.
69   All the judges who heard the case considered these alternative interpretations. Bennion in 'Hansard: Help or Hindrance', 1993 Stat. LR 149, takes a different view that 'a proper proportion' left a discretion to the Revenue. On this view the Minister's statement was just an explanation as to how the Revenue would exercise its discretion.
70   See Tunkel, 1993 *Taxation* 392; Lyell, '*Pepper v Hart* The Government Perspective', 15 Stat. LR 1 using the example of the complicated background to the case itself at p. 3–5, and Williams, 'The Finance Act 1993: Incredible Drafting', 1993 *BTR* 483.
71   'What Price Hansard?' Lord Lester, Hansard Society; it is also beyond the reach of many university libraries.
72   Whiteman on Income Tax 1–58.
73   1993 STC 624 at 629. See discussion in Bates, 'Parliamentary Material and Statutory Construction: Aspects of the Practical Approach to *Pepper v Hart*', 14 *Stat. LR* 46 at 51.
74   Williams, 'Taxing Statutes are Taxing Statutes: the Interpretation of Revenue Legislation', 1978 *MLR* 404; see also Hansard Report para 226.

75   [1994] 3 All ER 736.
76   See Zander, *The Law-Making Process* (4th ed., 1994), p. 155.
77   Williams, 'The Finance Act 1993: Incredible drafting, extraordinary prose', 1993 BTR 483 at p. 484.
78   [1993] 1 All ER 42 at p. 64 j.
79   Miers, 'Taxing Perks and Interpreting Statutes: *Pepper v Hart*', 1993 *MLR* 695 at 706–7.
80   Jenkins, '*Pepper v Hart*. A Draftsman's Perspective', 1994 15 Stat. LR 23.
81   At p. 63 j. See also Lord Lester, '*Pepper v Hart* Revisited', Stat. LR 10 and papers deposited by him in the Manuscripts Library at UCL.
82   At p. 50 b.
83   At p. 65 c.
84   See Bell and Engle, *Cross on Statutory Interpretation* (3rd edn. 1995) at p. 220.
85   Usher, 'The Impact of EEC Legislation on the UK courts', 1989 *Stat. LR* 95 at 109.
86   'Rules of Interpretation of EEC Legislation' [1989] *Stat. LR* 163.
87   Now eleven languages.
88   Neville Brown and Kennedy classify the methods into four: literal, historical, contextual and teleological. See *The Court of Justice of the European Communities*, 1994 at p. 301.
89   Ibid. at p. 318.
90   'British Statutory Interpretation in the Light of Community and Other International Obligations', Rensen, 1993 14 *Stat. LR* 186.
91   [1988] 2 All ER 922.
92   At p. 933, Advocate General.
93   *The Court of Justice of the European Communities*, 1994, at p. 321.
94   The Presiding Special Commissioner and Chairman of the VAT Tribunals said at the IFS Conference on Purposive Tax Legislation, 'We, the Tribunals, have found it relatively easy to work in the European dimension'.
95   [1992] 4 All ER 929 at 939.
96   1995 STC 239.
97   See 'The Law of Taxation in a European Environment', Tiley, 1992 *CLJ* 451.
98   This is acknowledged but seen as unrealistic in the Inland Revenue report, 'The Path to Tax Simplification', 1995, paras. 14–18.
99   1994 BTR 380; see also 'Pruning the Triffid', Ernst and Young 1994.
100   14 *Fiscal Studies* 95 at 103.
101   'The Role of the Law Commission in Simplifying Statute Law', 1995 16 *Stat. LR* 1.
102   Inland Revenue, 'The Path to Tax Simplification', December 1995, and the background paper.
103   Inland Revenue, 'Tax Law Rewrite', July 1996. Inland Revenue Press Release, 11 October 1996, gives further examples of rewritten tax legislation.
104   Report of the Working Party on the Reorganisation of the Income Tax Act 1976, the Valabh Report, September 1993. 'The Path to Tax Simplification' background paper Annex 3 contains useful information about tax simplification in other countries.
105   For an example of the demand for such a project, see Wajsbrem, 'Taxation Reform: A New Agenda for the Nineties', 1992 ATR 140.
106   See Barlow in IFS Conference on Purposive Tax Legislation.
107   1994 ATR 61 and 1995 ATR 75.
108   'The Finance Bill Process', 1995 *BTR* 33. 'The Right Path to Tax Simplification', 1996 *BTR* 1.
109   *Fiscal Studies* (1996) vol. 17, no. 3 63

110   Hansard Report paras 245–252.
111   See Discussion in Avery-Jones, *Fiscal Studies* (1996) vol. 17, no. 3 63 at 73.
112   The notes on clauses were published for the first time last year.

5 Interpreting Children's Legislation

Michael Freeman

This is an examination of the way judges interpret children's legislation. Three statutes are considered: the Children Act 1989, the Child Abduction and Custody Act 1985 and the Family Law Reform Act 1969 (though only one provision of this – section 8 – is examined). The statutes have different provenances: the Children Act a multiplicity of sources,[1] the Abduction statute two international conventions,[2] the Family Law Reform Act a committee of inquiry into the age of majority chaired by a judge.[3] The Children Act is accompanied by nine volumes of departmental guidance:[4] its implementation was preceded by a semi-official commentary.[5] It was debated at length, both in and out of Parliament,[6] and those who were to administer it were intensively trained. This cannot be said of other legislative provisions which are the subject of this article. The abduction legislation is in operation in a large number of other countries,[7] so that courts outside England have had to grapple with the same interpretational problems: there is thus a wealth of comparative experience.[8] Judges can thus look to foreign precedents: this is relatively rare and is not the case with the other statutes in focus.

This chapter is not a detailed examination of the case law. It is necessarily selective. Its concern is to uncover how judges approach a particular genre of legislation. Litigation concerned with children has features lacking elsewhere. The rhetoric of welfare is all-pervasive.[9] But where do judges get their understanding of this from? And how do they interpret it in the context of different pieces of legislation, where the policy objectives diverge, as they do in the three Acts? What techniques are employed? In a post-*Pepper v Hart*[10] world, what recourse is there to extrinsic material? Does an image of childhood emerge? Does the judicial approach to children throw any light upon the way society constructs childhood or adult–child relations in England at the end of the twentieth century?[11] These are important, and neg-

65

lected, questions. The answers may throw as much light on the craft[12] of judging as they do on the concept of childhood.

The Children Act 1989

A number of statements in the early days of the 1989 Act throw light on how in general terms the judiciary saw the Act and its role under it. Children Act litigation was said to be not 'ordinary civil litigation'. It concerns children where it is 'often necessary to subjugate justice to the adults to the interests of the children'.[13] The proceedings were said to be 'not paternal, not administrative and not in reality non-adversarial', though they were to be conducted in a non-adversarial spirit. They were 'adversarial', however, in the sense that each party was 'entitled to be heard and to challenge opposing evidence in cross-examination and to be represented'.[14] The Act was said to have the 'aim' of incorporating the 'best of wardship jurisdiction within the statutory framework without any of the perceived disadvantages of judicial monitoring of administrative plans'.[15]

The Master of the Rolls[16] was quick to seize on a conflict of ideologies in the Act between the child as subject and the child as legitimate 'object' of concern.[17] He thought the Act enabled a 'judicious balance to be struck between [these] two considerations'. First, there was, he said:

> the principle, to be honoured and respected, that children are human beings, in their own right with individual minds and wills, views and emotions, which should command serious attention. The second is the fact that a child is, after all, a child. The reason why the law is particularly solicitous in protecting the interests of children is because they are liable to be vulnerable and impressionable, lacking the maturity to weigh the longer term against the shorter, lacking the insight to know how they will react, and the imagination to know how others will react in certain situations, lacking the experience to measure the probable against the possible.[18]

Butler-Sloss L.J., one of the Act's progenitors,[19] also emphasized the way the Act recognized the integrity and personality of the child without totally endorsing children's rights. 'The whole purpose of the Children Act', she said, 'is not to hand over the children like packages or pieces of property'. But lest it be thought she was substituting an image of the child as an autonomous being, she added that 'we have not moved into the age of child power'.[20] She used similar imagery in another case also reported in 1992. Children, she said, 'should not be treated as packages and removed from one place to another and back again because grown-ups are involved in a dispute and have overlooked that children have rights'.[21]

The Children Act states that, when a court determines any question with respect to the 'upbringing of a child,'[22] the child's welfare is the paramount consideration.[23] This, together with the welfare checklist,[24] which puts bones on the flesh of an abstract principle, and the minimal intervention directive in section 1(5), may be thought to be the keys to understanding the Act.

How, then, have the judges interpreted the paramountcy principle? They have had no difficulty in ruling on the meaning of 'paramount',[25] but they have had problems identifying its scope. The Act itself offers little assistance: using a technique more akin to a continental legislative draftsman, it offers a framework but few details. Thus, it does not spell out what is meant by 'upbringing' and, although it purports to extend to 'any question', does it/can it really mean this? Thus, the courts have had to grapple with such questions as whether the paramountcy principle governs an application for a parental responsibility order,[26] an application by a local authority for a secure accommodation order,[27] an application for leave to apply for a section 8 order,[28] an application for an ouster order.[29] Although the first of these relates to an unmarried father's status, rather than the upbringing of a child, twice[30] the Court of Appeal has been prepared to 'accept' or 'assume'[31] that whether or not a father should have a parental responsibility order requires the judge to adopt the welfare principle as the paramount consideration. Balcombe L.J., who gave the main judgment in both cases, sought succour in the first of them in the knowledge that authority establishes that, 'other things being equal, it is always to a child's welfare to know, and wherever possible, to have contact with both its parents'.[32]

This is a conclusion from which few would dissent, and yet in other questions where status is in issue such as adoption the child's welfare is not (or not yet)[33] paramount[34] and in others, the parental order which may be granted to gamete donors,[35] there is no reference to the child's welfare at all.

What is striking is that the Court of Appeal has been prepared to construe 'a question' relating to 'upbringing' widely in this context, but not do so in relation to any of the other three applications for orders referred to above.[36] The Court of Appeal's reasoning[37] for refusing to allow an application for a secure accommodation order[38] to be constrained by the paramountcy principle was two-fold. As Butler-Sloss L.J. put it:

> the framework of Part III of the Act is structured to cast upon the local authority duties and responsibilities for children in its area and being looked after. The general duty of a local authority to safeguard and promote the child's welfare is not the same as that imposed upon the court in s. 1(1) placing welfare as the paramount consideration ... . Among those duties and powers is the right of a local authority to hold a child in secure accommodation for up to 72 hours without a court order. To be enabled to do so the local authority has to surmount

the hurdle of the requirements of s. 25(1) ... . In coming to the decision to restrict the liberty of a child the local authority will also have regard to their duty to safeguard and promote the welfare of a child who is looked after by them (s. 22(3)). The welfare principle is rightly to be considered by the local authority in coming to so serious and Draconian decision as the restriction upon the liberty of the child. They have the power, however, to place him in secure accommodation if he is likely to injure others rather than himself (s. 25(1)(b)). This power may be inconsistent with the concept of the child's welfare being paramount.[39]

Secondly, although 'it might reasonably be argued that a s. 25 application comes within the definition of a "question with respect to the upbringing of the child"', ... 'the wording of s. 1' is 'either irrelevant to or inconsistent with s. 25. The paramountcy principle is inconsistent with the duties of the local authority and with s. 25 (1)(b)'.[40] She concluded that 'the welfare of the child is of great importance and must take its place in the relevant criteria'.[41] But 'at the end of the day' if these were satisfied, there was a 'mandatory requirement' that the court made an order authorizing the child be kept in secure accommodation.[42]

This was not the view of Douglas Brown J.,[43] though two other first instance judges[44] had reached similar conclusions to what the Court of Appeal has now held to be the law. Of the commentators on the Children Act three – Masson,[45] Bainham[46] and White, Carr and Lowe[47] – totally ignored the question: I discussed it but came to the conclusion, wrongly it now seems, that the paramountcy requirement did govern secure accommodation applications.[48] No assistance can be obtained from *travaux préparatoires* but the Department of Health *Guidance and Regulations* is clear: 'The court must ... be satisfied that the order will positively contribute to the child's welfare and must not make an order unless it considers that doing so would be better for the child than making an order at all'.[49] Butler-Sloss L.J., as indicated, disagrees. This she is perfectly entitled to do: *Guidance* guides; it does not constrain. But the message is clear: with troublesome youth 'welfare' is to take a back seat to other considerations. Provisions are to be construed narrowly where other matters of greater importance (as perceived by the judiciary) are in conflict.

The courts have also held that applications for leave to apply for a section 8 order – at least where applications are made by an adult – are not governed by s. 1(1). The reason, according to Balcombe L.J., is that in granting or refusing an application for leave to apply for a section 8 order, the court is not determining a question with respect to the upbringing of the child concerned. That question only arises when the court hears the substantive application.[50] The court argued, using not dissimilar logic from *Re M*,[51] that some of the criteria in s. 10(9) which had to guide the court would be otiose if the whole matter were subject to the overriding provision in s. 1(1). But can a court ignore matters of substance when considering an application for leave? It has been admitted[52] that, when considering one of the matters to which it is required to have regard when determining whether to grant leave, namely 'any risk there might be of the proposed application disrupting the child's life to such an extent that he would be harmed by it',[53] the court is inevitably drawn into considering matters of substance.

If the paramountcy principle is not to govern an application for leave by an adult, should it where the application is by a child? The criteria in s. 10(9), to which reference has been made, do not apply where the applicant is the child.[54] The Act only structures child applications by insisting as a pre-condition that the court first be satisfied that the child has 'sufficient understanding' to make the proposed application.[55] But it lays down no criteria to govern the application for leave. Is it a lacuna in the statute (in which case how should it be filled?) or is the intention that courts should see the paramountcy provision as the governing principle? Again, there is no guidance in the *travaux préparatoires* or in the Department of Health literature.

There are three first instance judgments: two[56] hold that the child's welfare is not the paramount consideration; one[57] holds that it is. There is an emerging consensus (again the matter was ignored in the original commentaries) that the first view is the correct one.[58] It treats children in the same way as adults and accords children with sufficient understanding 'some degree of independence which seems more in keeping with the spirit of the Act'.[59] But, aside from the fact that this is only partially true,[60] what this view overlooks is that these applications are made by troubled children who are seeking help. To distinguish leave from the substantive application in such a way as to withdraw welfare paramountcy concerns from the former is not only artificial, but may well fail those children who need these concerns to be addressed. And, of course, if a parent, confronted by a child about to apply for a residence order because he wanted to leave home, were to make the child a ward of court, the child's welfare would become the paramount consideration.[61] Where there are gaps in legislation as here, surely a useful point of departure are the general principles set out in it?

The courts have held too – though here less controversially – that an application by a spouse[62] to exclude the other from the matrimonial home does not relate to the upbringing of their children and so is not determined by the paramountcy principle. It was the House of Lords in 1983 in *Richards v Richards*[63] which scotched any conjecture that ouster applications should be governed by the paramountcy principle.[64] But there was always a chance however slim that a court would construe s. 1(1) as governing such an application. The argument that s. 1(1) had overruled *Richards v Richards* was cursorily dismissed as 'hopeless' by Nourse L.J.[65] Said Balcombe L.J.:

'If it had been the intention of Parliament to reverse ... *Richards v Richards* in relation to ordinary ouster applications I am quite certain they would have said so expressly.'[66] It is, I think, a stronger argument than these judges were prepared to credit, and, given the technique employed in the Act, it was no more likely that it would refer to the applicability of the paramountcy principle to ouster applications than to anything else. Where husband/father lives is, it may be argued, certainly a question directly relating to the upbringing of children.

It is difficult to conclude from an analysis of these 'hard cases' on paramountcy that the judges have a coherent philosophy of interpretation. In the parental responsibility order case[67] the court's response is intuitive, rather than reasoned. It gives effect to what the court understands as commonsense policy ('always a child's welfare to know ... both its parents').[68]

The secure accommodation cases[69] seem a more blatant example of favouring an interpretation which may assist the implementation of a particular policy. Without specifically invoking the 'mischief' rule, it is as if the court is saying 'what can we do to ensure troublesome youngsters are restrained?' Over-reliance on the principles of section 1 could obstruct this goal (note Butler-Sloss L.J.'s remark that it was 'probable that the wishes and feelings of M are inconsistent with the need for his sake to restrict his liberty').[70]

Both in this case (*Re M*) and in the cases on 'leave',[71] the courts have been at pains to put the provision under scrutiny into its textual criteria in s. 25 and, as regards adults seeking leave, in s. 10(9) as firm indications that Parliament had intended these provisions to stipulate exclusive governing considerations. But, in reaching the conclusion that s. 1(1) did not govern an application by a child for leave, this argument was not open, and recourse was sought instead in the logic of analogy between the two sorts of applicants. It may be thought that this is to prioritize logic over life.[72] It is difficult to see how the question whether a child should be given leave to pursue an application to change his or her residential arrangements is not a question relating to that child's upbringing.

The argument used in the fourth example (the ouster application)[73] that failure to refer specifically is clear evidence that Parliament did not intend to include and thereby change the law is one that is commonly proffered. It is an argument with some strength, but has less weight where the legislative technique under scrutiny (the paramountcy principle) provides a framework for interpretation rather than a set of detailed provisions.

The most difficult question that the courts have had to answer in relation to the paramountcy principle concerns whose welfare is paramount where there is more than one child. The problem first surfaced in a case where both mother and child were under eighteen:[74] it has since commanded attention where the interests of siblings did not coincide.[75] The latter problem was anticipated by the Law Commission:[76] surprisingly, the former was not. In *Birmingham City Council v H*[77] (where stopping contact[78] between a 15-year-old mother and her small son was the issue and this would enhance the welfare of the latter but not the former), Balcombe L.J. in the Court of Appeal noted the Law Commission's solution but also the fact that 'for whatever reason, the draftsman of the 1989 Act did not adopt [this]'. Accordingly, he said, 'we have to resolve the dilemma ourselves'.[79]

The question is such an obvious one that it is surprising that Parliament did not attempt a solution. Is the omission a genuine oversight or an acknowledgement that a solution can be best forged in the heat and pragmatism of real-life litigation? Only White, Carr and Lowe, of the commentators on the Act, alluded to the problem, but they too failed to grapple with the thorniest of the problems which occurs where both parent and child are children.[80]

At first instance Connell J. held that the baby's welfare was the paramount consideration and that, since contact was the right of the child and not that of the parent,[81] the baby's welfare took priority over the mother's. The Court of Appeal disagreed.[82] Taking the view that the question of contact with the mother related to the upbringing of the baby, it held that, while the welfare of both taken together should be considered as paramount to the interests of any adults concerned in their lives, as between themselves the court should approach the question of their welfare without giving one priority over the other.[83]

The Court of Appeal saw itself faced with 'an impossibility'.[84] In such a situation it saw its task as to 'give the statutory provision such meaning as it can sensibly bear, having regard to any other provisions of the Act which may throw light on the intention of the legislature'.[85] It did this by analysing the contact provisions in section 34. Although Evans L.J.'s attention also focused on these, he was equally concerned that the 'manifest objects'[86] were achieved. But this, in the context of the dilemma raised by this provision, only begs the question.

The House of Lords rejected the Court of Appeal's reasoning.[87] In a rather cursory one-judgment ruling, it confined its observations to the application of the contact provision (and to s. 34(4) in particular) and held that it is the child in respect of whom the application is being made – in this case the baby – whose interests are paramount. But it expressly left open the more general question 'as to whether an application by a parent who is a child for contact with its own child could be a question with respect to the "upbringing" of the child who is a parent or whether that question related only to the child's position as a parent and not to its "upbringing"'.[88] The Lords' reasoning has been, and can be justifiably, criticized for its narrowness and because the answer to which one comes will depend upon how the issue is framed, upon how the application is made.[89] But it does, unlike the decision of the Court of Appeal, offer a solution.

The *Birmingham* decision was followed in *F v Leeds City Council*[90] (in which case a baby had been removed from a 17-year-old mother within hours of the birth). Again, the court's approach was to identify which child was the subject of the application, and which child it was whose welfare was directly involved.[91] The answer in this case was clear since it was the baby, and not the child's mother, with respect to whom the application was being made and who was thus the subject of the application, and the only child to be named in the order. No question relating to the mother's upbringing arose: accordingly, there was no requirement to treat the mother's welfare as the paramount consideration.

The artificiality of this approach is clearly exemplified by the problem identified in *Re T and E*.[92] The interests of half-sisters were in conflict: it was in the interests of T for the care order to be revoked and a residence order made, allowing her to live with her father and his new family, but it was in the interests of E that both children should be placed together for adoption. It was Wall J.'s view, obiter, that:

> where a number of children are all the subject of an application or cross-application to the court in the same set of proceedings, and where it is impossible to achieve what is in the paramount interests of each child ... the balancing exercise described by the Court of Appeal in [the *Birmingham* case) has to be undertaken and the situation of least detriment to all the children achieved.[93]

Nor was this situation affected by the Lords' decision in the *Birmingham* case. However, in *Re T and E* there was only one application under the Children Act: T was the subject of this and on a 'strict' interpretation the paramountcy principle applied only to her. The other application was to free the children for adoption: that application was governed by another Act, the Adoption Act, where the children's welfare was the first, but not the paramount, consideration.[94] T's welfare was paramount and therefore had to prevail. Wall J. observed how unsatisfactory it was that the vital question of children's welfare should depend upon the vagaries[95] of procedure, and the timing of different applications.

Of these three cases it is only the last in which the Law Commission's formulation 'any child likely to be affected' in the welfare equation[96] would have made any difference. Wall J. referred to it[97] but, noting that Parliament had rejected it, was of the opinion that 'it would be wrong for me to achieve the same result by the back door'.[98]

Given the preparation that went into the Children Act, it is surprising how many problems which the courts have encountered were not anticipated.

Another, which was not, is vividly illustrated by the so-called 'Nottingham' decision.[99] The Children Act may be read as legislation which sets its face against heavy-handed surveillance of families.[100] Thus, the threshold for intervention is 'significant harm'[101] and recourse by local authorities to the inherent jurisdiction of the courts is discouraged.[102] The local authority in the *Nottingham* case, apparently like a number of other authorities, took the view that to implement this ideology, 'to avoid excessive intervention in the life of the family',[103] you used the private law route where this was possible. It may, of course, be queried whether it makes any difference to a family which route is taken, if the end result is intervention, particularly if it leads to the forced removal of a family member. But this is not my concern here.

In *Nottingham County Council*, following allegations of sexual abuse made against her father by the eldest daughter, the local authority obtained emergency protection orders in respect of two younger girls. It obstinately resisted judicial encouragement to apply for care or supervision orders[104] and instead applied for a prohibited steps order requiring the father neither to reside in the same household as the girls nor have any contact with them. The application was rejected. The President of the Family Division commented:

> This court should make it clear that the route chosen by the local authority…was wholly inappropriate. In cases where children are found to be at risk of suffering significant harm … a clear duty arises on the part of local authorities to take steps to protect them. In such circumstances a local authority is required to assume responsibility and to intervene in the family arrangements in order to protect the child.[105]

There is no power to oust an abuser in the Children Act. There could have been, but an amendment to introduce one was rejected during the passage of the Bill.[106] Reference was made to this in Sir Stephen Brown P.'s judgment.[107] There cannot be a clearer inference. However, the dissonance between the Act's ideology and the powers it contains remains. It is again striking that commentaries on the Act did not anticipate the problem in this case. Ward J., at first instance, admitted that he had not noticed that the Act had the effect of disabling local authorities and courts. 'Perhaps the lectures on the Children Act I have given and attended have so whet my appetite for the delights of the flexible range of practical remedies on the s. 8 "menu" that I totally forgot to ask myself whether it was right for me even to accept this invitation to dine at the private law table'.[108] But what are judges to do when Parliament purports to encode an ideology and sets up a structure which obstructs it?

In *Nottingham* they, rightly it is submitted, prioritized the structure over the ideology. The implication that some have drawn, however, namely, that a local authority can never use private law remedies has to be resisted. There is surely no reason why an authority, concerned at the excessive use of corporal punishment by a parent, should have to use public law remedies or any reason why a prohibited steps order should not be granted.

The trigger for compulsory intervention into the family is 'significant harm'.[109] In determining the meaning of this there is considerable interpretational latitude. But how much? The courts face a problem: a narrow interpretation may leave children unprotected; an unduly wide construction may extend the law beyond the scope of the mischief it is designed to address. The tension between a literal and a purposive approach to the construction of the care provision was at the centre of a remark of the President of the Family Division in *Newham London Borough v A.G.*.[110] He commented:

> I very much hope that in approaching cases under the Children Act 1989 courts will not be invited to perform in every case a strict legalistic analysis of the statutory meaning of s. 31. Of course, the words of the statute must be considered, but I do not believe that Parliament intended them to be unduly restrictive when the evidence clearly indicates that a certain course should be taken in order to protect the child.[111]

This impatience with legislative language is understandable, but it flies in the face of what Parliament, rightly or wrongly, was trying to do in imposing a threshold test and closing off the avenue of wardship. And imagine the reaction to this language and this advice had it occurred in relation to criminal legislation or a tax statute.

Problems of statutory construction in care legislation continued in *Re M*.[112] Speaking in the House of Lords, Lord Templeman, in language reminiscent of the President's, saw the appeal as 'an illustration of the tyranny of language and the importance of ascertaining and giving effect to the intentions of Parliament by construing a statute in accordance with the spirit rather than the letter of the Act'.[113] The case centred on the meaning of 'is suffering' in s. 31(2) of the 1989 Act. Bracewell J. ruled that the relevant date for deciding whether a child 'is suffering' significant harm relates to the period immediately before the process of protecting the child is first put into motion.[114] The Court of Appeal disagreed. Balcombe L.J. said the choice by Parliament of the phrase 'is suffering' over 'has suffered' (which was in the original draft of the Bill) emphasized the intention that it was not the past but the continuous present to which attention had to be directed. He concluded that it was not enough that something happened in the past which caused the child to suffer harm if, before the hearing, the child had ceased to suffer such harm.[115] The child had suffered significant harm but, in the

Court of Appeal's view, 16 months on and in the care of a good foster mother, was no longer suffering such harm, and was, therefore, outside the statutory requirement for a care order. The House of Lords did not agree.[116] Lord Mackay ruled that 'the relevant date with respect to which the court must be satisfied is the date at which the local authority initiated the procedure for protection'.[117] Although the child was not likely to suffer further significant harm, the House of Lords, rather surprisingly, made the care order it held it had the jurisdiction to make. Lord Mackay reasoned that there was a possibility in the longer term of difficulties, and the care order would enable the local authority to monitor the child's progress.[118] The decision looks wrong both as a matter of interpretation of the language of s. 31(2) and, in terms of the ideology of the Act, as a matter of social policy. But most commentators have approved the decision of the House of Lords.[119]

It says much about the difficulties of interpretation that both the decisions of the Court of Appeal and that of the House of Lords should give rise to concerns. As far as the Court of Appeal's decision is concerned, there was anxiety that it would undercut local authorities' abilities to protect children (if a relative was looking after a child, could it be said that the child was suffering or likely to suffer significant harm?). Another effect of the Court of Appeal's decision was to suppress the child's voice where, after removal from his parents, he is cared for by relatives. Since the local authority could not, according to the Court of Appeal, institute care proceedings, no guardian *ad litem* could be appointed to represent the child's interests, and there could be no independent inquiry into whether a care order is needed or not. The House of Lords' decision was equally flawed. Its interpretation enabled a care order to be made in circumstances not intended by the legislature or necessary on the facts of this case. Further, by refusing the relative a residence order it expected her to bring up the child without parental responsibility being vested in her. The Lords' decision left the local authority and the father (in prison for murdering the mother) with parental authority: to say, as the Lords did, that the local authority could control the way the father exercised his parental authority,[120] though true, was fatuous, given he would play no part in the child's life at all.

The final example on the Children Act is also a decision of the House of Lords, though on this occasion not a unanimous one. *Re H and R*[121] also centres on the interpretation of s. 31, but this time not on the meaning of 'is suffering', but on 'likely to suffer'. The courts have had to interpret the word 'likely' many times in other contexts.[122] Indeed, when they first confronted the problem in a Children Act case – *Newham London Borough v A.G.*[123] – the President of the Family Division quoted from, and approved, a judgment of Lord Reid in a Fatal Accidents Act claim.[124] That case hinged on the question whether an adulterous wife who had deserted her husband was likely to be reconciled with him. He had been killed in an accident and she wanted compensation. Lord Reid said:

> You can prove that a past event happened, but you cannot prove that a future event will happen and I do not think that the law is so foolish as to suppose that you can. All that you can do is to evaluate the chance. Sometimes it is virtually 100%: sometimes virtually nil. But often it is somewhere in between. And if it is somewhere in between I do not see much difference between a probability of 51% and 49%.[125]

Sir Stephen Brown P., following this line of argument, concluded that the interpretation of s. 31(2) in the Children Act should not be approached on the basis that 'likely to suffer' should be equated with 'on the balance of probabilities'. The court, he said, when looking to the future could only evaluate the chances.[126]

The House of Lords in *Re H and R* has now held that 'likely' is being used in the sense of a real possibility, a possibility that could not sensibly be ignored, having regard to the nature and gravity of the feared harm in the particular case.[127] In this case a step-father[128] had been acquitted of rape of his eldest step-daughter. Court orders were sought for the other three girls. They were refused by the judge who could not be sure 'to the requisite high standard of proof'[129] that the rape allegations were true. The Court of Appeal agreed, though there was a powerful dissenting judgment.[130] In its view, it was not open to the judge, once he had rejected the only allegation which gave rise to the applications, to go on to a second stage and consider the likelihood of future harm to the children.

The Lords agreed, but only in the face of two dissenting judgments.[131] Unresolved doubts and suspicions could, the majority held, no more form the basis of a conclusion that children were likely to suffer significant harm than they could form the basis on a conclusion that children are suffering such harm. But it was open to a court to conclude that there was a real possibility that a child would suffer harm in the future although harm in the past had not been established. There would be cases where, although the alleged maltreatment was not proved, the evidence did establish a combination of profoundly worrying features affecting the care of the child within the family: in such cases, it would be open to a court in appropriate circumstances to find that, although not satisfied that the child was yet suffering significant harm, on the basis of such facts as were proved there was a likelihood that s/he would do so in the future.

Lord Nicholls saw the Lords' decision as an attempt to balance interests of children and parents.[132] But he also accepted that 'the more improbable the event, the stronger must be the evidence that it did occur before, on the balance of probability, its occurrence will be established'.[133] There is some irony in this, which seems to have escaped their Lordships' notice, that, as the anticipated injury becomes more serious, the more difficult it becomes to protect the child.

The decision has caused concern. It will lead to fewer cases being taken to court and those which do will need to have been thoroughly investigated. But, if fewer cases are to be taken to court, there will need to be greater emphasis on partnership,[134] on working with families. However, for these cases which are destined for court, the work involved to get the case up to the standards required may obstruct the very work with families and their co-operation which will be essential to the child's well-being if the threshold condition for care is not met. One is led to wonder whether the House of Lords, engrossed as it was in the logic of interpretation, really appreciated the consequences of its decision.

The Child Abduction and Custody Act 1985

The abduction of a child is a hangover from the concept of the child as 'property'.[135] Two international conventions, one from the Council of Europe, the other the Hague Convention, have attempted to tackle the problem of international child abduction. The United Kingdom is a signatory to both conventions and both are incorporated in the 1985 Act. Only the Hague Convention (which covers more countries and can be invoked where there is no court order) is considered in this article, but both conventions have similar aims, namely to return abducted children promptly to home countries so that any dispute as to their care can be determined there. The conventions set their faces against abductors gaining any tactical advantage from the abduction. They can also be seen as intended to deter abductions. There is, accordingly, a presumption in favour of returning the child, and a reluctance to investigate the merits of disputes over residence and upbringing.

In Children Act proceedings, at least those which relate to a child's upbringing,[136] the child's welfare is paramount.[137] But, in the context of the Hague Convention, the courts have interpreted welfare as congruent with restoring the child to his/her home environment. A striking illustration of this is the case of *N v N*.[138] The mother had abducted[139] the three children from Australia. In the words of the judge: 'The mother is seeking to obliterate the father from her life and the lives of the children, almost as though he were dead. If she succeeds in distancing him by ten thousand or more miles, directly or indirectly discouraging contact, what will be the long-term effect on the children of losing a devoted father in such a way?'[140] There was evidence, though the court thought this should be evaluated in Australia, that this 'devoted' father had sexually abused one of the children (the 8-year-old daughter). The court held that it had to weigh the psychological harm of returning the children against the psychological consequences of refusing return. Given that both risks were substantial, the court held that it had to speculate which was the more substantial and 'in exercising the discretion in such circumstances, due weight [had to] be given to the important primary purpose of the Convention to ensure the swift return of abducted children'.[141] The welfare of children was said to be important, but not a paramount consideration.[142]

The only reference in the Convention (and thus the Act) to children's welfare is found in one of the section 13 defences (which was an issue in *N v N*). To read welfare as important rather than paramount is thus a judicial construction rather than a literal reading of the legislative act. But it is necessary if the underlying objectives of the Convention are to be carried through. And so committed are the courts to these that they have held[143] that the principles underlying the Conventions are so important that it is the duty of the court to consider taking steps to secure that a parent is informed of his or her rights under them. This is an unusual exercise of paternalism, to say the least. In Children Act cases, where paramountcy is the guiding principle, the courts are concerned with the best interests of the child whose upbringing is in question. But Convention cases are concerned not just with the interests of the abducted children in the case before it, but with the interests of abducted children generally.[144]

The Hague Convention can only be activated where a child has been wrongfully removed to, or retained in, another contracting state.[145] 'Wrongful' means that the action was in breach of rights of custody attributed to a person, institution or any other body and that, at the time of the removal or retention, those rights were actually being exercised jointly or alone, or would have been but for the removal or retention.[146] The House of Lords has put a narrow interpretation on 'removal' and 'retention'. They are both, it has held, single events, so that if a child is wrongfully removed before the Convention came into force but not returned after that date such latter conduct does not constitute 'retention' within the meaning of the Convention.[147] The two concepts are mutually exclusive. 'Removal occurs when a child, which has previously been in the state of its habitual residence, is taken across the frontier of that state; whereas retention occurs where a child, which has previously been for a limited period outside the state of its habitual residence, is not returned to that state on the expiry of such limited period'.[148]

'Wrongful' has, however, been construed broadly. In *Re C*,[149] there was a consent order made by a court in Sydney, giving the mother custody, a clause of which prescribed that neither father nor mother 'shall remove the child from Australia without the consent of the other'. The mother removed the child to England without such consent. It was held that the father's right amounted to a right of custody,[150] enabling him to decide whether, at the request of the mother, the child should live inside or outside Australia. In *C v C*[151] it was held that a removal might be 'wrongful' where there was no declaration from the relevant foreign court (in this case New York State). The English court was prepared to rely upon a line of New York case law, which was authority for the proposition that an award of visitation rights created 'an implied prohibition running against the custodial parent removing the child to a distant place, which would frustrate regular visitation and render the non-custodial parent's rights nugatory'.[152]

The Convention applies to any child who was 'habitually resident in a Contracting State immediately before any breach of custody or access rights'.[153] 'Habitual residence' is a concept used in many statutes, most of which derive from Hague conventions, but in no statute is it defined. Not surprisingly, this has caused problems. The courts have held it is possible to have no habitual residence,[154] but they have gone to extremes to avoid this conclusion. Thus, in *V v B*,[155] two months in New South Wales, and in *Re F*,[156] a month in Queensland with 'settled intention'[157] were held sufficient periods of time to establish habitual residence. Butler-Sloss L.J. explicitly recognized the importance for the successful operation of the Hague Convention that, where possible, a child should have a habitual residence. In *Re E*,[158] the Court of Appeal went further and ruled that there is a presumption in favour of the continuance of an existing habitual residence, and that the burden of proving a change of habitual residence lies on the party so asserting.

Habitual residence is a matter of fact:[159] it is not a 'metaphysical legal concept'.[160] The Court of Appeal held[161] that it could not be acquired by a child who was not physically resident in the country concerned. Nor can a parent with joint parental responsibility change a child's habitual residence without the other parent's consent. It had to follow that a mere decision on her part could not change the child's habitual residence. It has also been held[162] that a child can have more than one habitual residence, though since these had to be consecutive and not concurrent, s/he could not be habitually resident in more than one place at the same time. A consequence of this is that where a child has two homes (in *Re V* in Corfu and London), the failure by a parent to return children at the agreed date to the parent at the other home did not come within the Convention. A premium is thus put on proving that the jurisdiction in which the child is retained is not that child's habitual residence.[163]

The most contentious part of the Convention – and the Article which caused most interpretational problems both in England and elsewhere – is the packages of 'defences' to international child abduction in Article 13. The 'message' of the Convention is clear and the English courts comply with it. So they 'set their face against the removal of the child'.[164] This should have led to Article 13 being construed strictly. However, the courts have not been consistent.

The courts may refuse to return a child where the parent from whom the child was abducted 'was not actually exercising the custody rights at the time of removal or retention'. Where there is consent, the evidence to establish it needs to be 'clear and compelling'.[165] Even where there has been consent, it does not follow that the child will not be returned. Thus, in *Re K*,[166] where there was consent and more than 12 months elapsed, the court still returned the child to Texas from where he came. He was, said the court, a Texan child of Texan parents and the claims of the Texan jurisdiction to decide his future were accordingly overwhelming. Texas was, the court concluded, the *forum conveniens*.[167]

The concept of 'acquiescence' is difficult and has troubled the courts. It has been interpreted widely, arguably to the detriment of the parent from whom the child has been taken. Thus, in *Re A*,[168] a letter written immediately after the abduction which said 'I'm not going to fight it. I am going to sacrifice myself rather than [the boys]' was held incapable of any construction other than a clearly expressed acquiescence. Stuart-Smith L.J. said that a party cannot be said to acquiesce 'unless he is aware, at least in general terms, of his rights against the other parent'.[169] However, it is not necessary, so it was said, that he should know that full or precise nature of his legal rights, but he must be aware that the other parent's act in removing or retaining the child is unlawful. And if he is aware of the factual situation giving rise to those rights, the court will no doubt readily infer that he was aware of his legal rights, either if he could reasonably be expected to have known of them or taken steps to obtain legal advice. Acquiescence is not a continuing state of affairs: the question is whether, at some time, the parent acquiesced.

Nevertheless, the Vice-Chancellor,[170] interpreting 'acquiescence' in what he considered to be the underlying objectives of the Convention, has said that courts should be 'slow to infer acquiescence from conduct which is consistent with the parent ... accepting, as an ... emergency expedient only, a situation forced on him and which in practical terms he is unable to change at once'.[171] It was his view that the Convention has 'to be interpreted and applied having regard to the way responsible parents can be expected to behave'.[172] There was, as he saw it, a 'spectrum'[173] with two edges: at the one edge there was the parent who accepted that the abducted child should stay where he or she is for 'a matter of days or a week or two'; at the other edge 'the parent may ... accept that the child should stay where he or she is for an indefinite period, likely to be many months or longer'.[174] And here it is a question of degree. Knowledge of rights under the Convention is but one circumstance which would then need to be taken into account. In *Re S*[175] the Court of Appeal admitted that 'subjective analysis'[176] was not wholly excluded, though care had to be taken 'not to give undue emphasis'[177] to these elements. The central question was said to be: 'has the aggrieved parent conducted himself in a way that is inconsistent with his later seeking a summary return?'[178] Acquiescence must be clear and unequivocal.[179] This was said in a case in which Balcombe L.J. weighed alleged acquiescence in the balance 'against the policy of the Convention',[180] and this policy was deemed to be of greater weight. It has, however, been accepted that 'there is a vast difference between accepting a degree of blame for the breakdown of the marriage and acquiescing in the retention of the children abroad'.[181]

The court is also not bound to return a child if there is 'a grave risk that his or her return would expose the child to physical or psychological harm or otherwise place the child in an intolerable situation'.[182] There is only one reported English appellate case where this defence has succeeded.[183] This is the only provision in the Convention where the issue of the child's welfare can be legitimately raised, but the courts, aware as they are of the objectives of the Convention, have done their best to frustrate those who would invoke it. Thus, Bracewell J. in *Re N*[184] said: 'it is plain that it is not a trivial risk and it is not a trivial psychological harm which is envisaged and which has to be justified and, furthermore, I am satisfied that the intolerable situation envisaged has to be something extreme and compelling'.[185] In *P v P*,[186] the mother claimed that if the court ordered the return of the children to the USA she would become deeply unhappy and this would make the children unhappy too. The argument was said to be 'beside the point'. This was not because the courts were inhumane. 'On the contrary there is an humane purpose underlying it in ensuring that children are not subjected to disruption through arbitrary movement by one parent'.[187]

The courts have nevertheless accepted that psychological harm can include that suffered by the abducting parent. In *Re G*,[188] it was convinced that to return a child to Texas would lead to the mother's mental condition worsening and this would put the child at risk. There was evidence of depression and a prognosis that the mother might become psychotic. It has been accepted[189] that harm can include financial harm.

As has been seen, courts have returned children even where there is evidence that they may have been sexually abused.[190]

They have refused to listen to the argument that a child would be in danger if s/he returned unaccompanied. Thus, in *Re C*,[191] the mother said that she would refuse to accompany the child if he was returned to Australia.

It was her view that the child would therefore suffer severe psychological harm. The Court of Appeal rejected this argument: a parent cannot create a psychological situation and then seek to rely on it. In *Re L*[192] a baby of 18 months was returned to Texas in the face of evidence that the mother might not get a visa to accompany him and of affidavit evidence of two psychologists that to separate a mother from a child of this age would cause grave psychological harm. Hollis J. was of the view that, even if the mother failed to obtain a visa, the child would not be exposed to psychological harm because he would be cared for by his father and paternal grandmother. The father – because of the abduction – had not seen the child for six months, but the court was satisfied that the child knew his father and his paternal grandmother 'although less well than his father'.[193] The evidence for this is not clear. On the face of it this is an extraordinary decision, redolent of much-criticized cases in other contexts,[194] and one which could never be reached today outside the context of an international abduction.

The only reported appellate case in which the defence has succeeded (*Re F*[195]) was one in which there was evidence both of domestic violence and of physical abuse of the child.[196] This was the cause of nightmares and bedwetting. Additionally, the child was asthmatic. It was said that returning the child to the surroundings in which he had previously been not simply a witness to marital discord but a victim of it would, on the facts, create a grave risk that his return would expose him to psychological harm and would place him in an intolerable situation. Butler-Sloss L.J. admitted she reached this conclusion with 'considerable hesitation'.[197]

The Convention also allows the court to refuse to return the child in the face of that child's objections. The child has to have reached 'an age and degree of maturity at which it is appropriate to take account of its views'. The Court of Appeal has ruled that the child's objection is an entirely separate matter from paragraph (b) of Article 13, and that there is no need to establish that the child will be at risk of physical or psychological harm before the discretion comes into play.[198]

The Convention does not specify an age.[199] In *Re R*,[200] Balcombe L.J. was prepared to listen to the objections of a child of seven-and-a-half, though Millett L.J. was not. Seven seems to be the earliest age at which English courts have taken note of a child's objection.[201] What is required is not just 'instinct' but 'the discernment which a mature child brings to the question's implication for his or her best interests in the long and the short term'.[202] Often the child's objection will be to separation from the abducting parent rather than one to being returned to the home environment.[203] Often too the child's views will have been influenced by the abducting parent, and when the courts have deemed this to be so they have given little or no weight to those views.[204]

The meaning of 'objects' has also caused interpretational problems. Should the word be interpreted literally and, if not, what gloss should be put on the word? Bracewell J. in *Re R* thought that 'before the court can consider exercising discretion, there must be more than a mere preference expressed by the child. The word "objects" imparts a strength of feeling which goes far beyond the usual ascertainment of the wishes of the child in a custody dispute'.[205] But this view did not commend itself to Sir Stephen Brown P. in an unreported case,[206] and the Court of Appeal in *S v S*,[207] has taken the view that 'objects' should be interpreted literally, without imposing any gloss on the word at all.

Even if the child has reached the requisite level of maturity, his or her return can still be ordered.[208] The seven-year-old girl in the case in which this was said[209] appeared afraid to return to a home in which she recollected severe physical chastisement.[210] Where a child has expressed a wish to remain, the court has to decide how much weight to give to the child's views, bearing in mind the purposes of the Convention. Thus, in *S v S*[211] the court was alert to the danger that Article 13 could be interpreted in a manner which would undermine the notion that it is normally in the best interests of children that they should be promptly returned to the country from which they have been wrongfully removed. Note Balcombe L.J.'s remark in that case that to give effect to a child's views where these have been influenced by some other person would be 'to drive a coach and horses through the primary scheme of the Hague Convention'.[212] In *S v S* the court thought the nine-year-old's reasons for not wishing to be returned to France, that she found being educated in English easier, both independent and valid and upheld them.

The courts have applied Convention principles to non-Convention cases.[213] But in non-Convention cases the welfare of children is the paramount consideration.[214] Accordingly, 'the principles of the Convention are applicable only to the extent that they indicate what is normally in the interests of the children'.[215] There is concern that the courts are too willing to apply Hague principles to non-Convention cases. The courts have said that they will do so only where the non-Convention country applies principles not significantly different from that of English courts.[216] But in the case in which this was said (*Re S*[217]), children were returned to Pakistan where according to the expert evidence they could be deprived of the care of their mother if she remarried, formed a liaison with a man other than a close relative of the children, or if she was deemed to be unsuitable, for example if she lived an unIslamic way of life. The underlying assumption of the Convention is that 'the courts of all its signatories are equally concerned to ensure, and equally capable of ensuring, that both parties receive a fair hearing, and that all issues of child welfare receive a skilled, thorough and humane evaluation'.[218] The children in *Re S* were returned to a system whose principles are not compatible with the welfare standard cognizable in English courts. Comity may be at the root of the Convention:[219] it is more difficult to accept its application where the welfare of children is looked upon so differently.

The Family Law Reform Act 1969

The 1969 Act, following the Latey committee[220] report, lowered the age of majority from 21 to 18. It also in s. 8(1) provided in unambiguous language that 'the consent of a minor who has attained the age of sixteen ... shall be as effective as it would be if he were of full age'. This was pre-*Gillick*[221] as well as before the emphasis on a child's autonomy and participation in decision-making that is associated with the UN Convention[222] and the Children Act, both passed in 1989. But its intentions were clear and the import unquestioned, at least until the Court of Appeal came to decide *Re W* in 1992.[223] Lord Donaldson MR said in this case:

> The argument that J., or any other 16 or 17-year-old, can by refusing to consent to treatment veto the treatment notwithstanding that the doctor has the consent of someone who has parental responsibilities involves the proposition that s. 8 has the further effect of depriving such a person of the power to consent. It certainly does not say so.[224]

And in *Re R*,[225] he had argued that, although the 16-year-old had the right to consent, 'if he or she declines to do so or refuses consent can be given by someone else who had parental rights or responsibilities'.[226]

It is true that s. 8(1) does only refer to the power to give a consent and not to a refusal to do so. It does not as such create a power of veto in favour of the 16-year-old. But it is wrong to draw the conclusion that Lord Donaldson does for two reasons. First, Parliament did not consider and reject the power of veto, and may have been assumed to believe that consent embraced refusal. Secondly, in coming to this conclusion Lord Donaldson is overlooking s. 8(3). This states that: 'Nothing in this section shall be construed as making ineffective any consent which would have been effective if this section had not been enacted'.

This provision has long puzzled but whatever it means – and much academic commentary considered it was intended to preserve the right of a child under 16 to continue to be able to provide a valid consent[227] – it is surely wrong to interpret it, as Lord Donaldson did, to uphold the rights of those with parental responsibilities. If he were right, until the passing of the 1969 Act any treatment of anyone under 21 without parental consent must have been unlawful, a conclusion so utterly preposterous that it is difficult to imagine anyone contemplating it. In addition, the common law rights to which Lord Donaldson refers are rights which have 'dwindled'[228] to the point of yielding to the child's right to make his or her own decisions when of 'sufficient understanding and intelligence'.[229] Lord Scarman's language in the *Gillick* case[230] could not be clearer: 'the parental right to determine whether *or not* their minor child below the age of 16 will have medical treatment terminates if and when the child achieves a sufficient understanding and intelligence to enable him or her to understand fully what is proposed.'[231]

In the first of the two cases (*Re R*[232]), the Family Law Reform Act was not in issue since the child concerned was only 15.[233] There are nevertheless some *obiter* comments on its meaning. But in *Re W*[234] the child, who suffered from anorexia nervosa, was 16, so that s. 8 was directly in point. And in *Re W* Lord Donaldson MR invoked the Latey report as an aid to construction. He notes:

> The report ... records that all the professional bodies which gave evidence recommended that patients aged between 16 and 18 should be able to give an effective consent to treatment and all but the Medical Protection Society recommended that they should also be able to give an effective refusal. The point with which we are concerned was therefore well in the mind of the committee. It did not so recommend. It recommended that '*without prejudice to any consent that may otherwise be lawful*, the consent of young persons aged 16 and over to medical or dental treatment shall be as valid as the consent of a person of full age'.[235]

Lord Donaldson MR could not accept that 'in adopting somewhat more prolix language' Parliament was 'intending to achieve a result which differed from that recommended by the committee'.[236] But he is surely reading too much into what the Latey committee recommended (as well as attaching too much significance to it). One would not have expected either the Latey committee or the 1969 Act to have added 'refusal to consent'. This was clearly implied and, in relation to *Gillick*-competence, made clear by Lord Scarman. He referred to the 'parental right to determine whether *or not* their minor child below the age of 16 will have medical treatment' terminating 'if and when the child achieves a sufficient understanding and intelligence to enable him or her to understand fully what is proposed'.[237] Lord Donaldson refers to the statement but what he says apropos of it is far from convincing:

> Lord Scarman was discussing the parents' right 'to *determine* whether or not their minor child below the age of 16 will have medical treatment', and this is the 'parental right' to which he was referring. A right of determination is wider than a right to consent. The parents can only have a right of determination if

either the child has no right to consent … *or* the parents hold a master-key which could nullify the child's consent. I do not understand Lord Scarman to be saying that, if a child was '*Gillick*-competent' … the parents ceased to have an independent right of consent, as contrasted with ceasing to have a right of determination, i.e. a veto.[238]

It is apparent that the Court of Appeal in these two cases have been more concerned to protect the medical profession than to recognize the scope of a child's autonomy.[239] What the court fails to see, or address, is how removing the legitimate expectations from rights-conscious adolescents is likely to provoke litigation. Extending this reasoning to 16-year-olds, a generation after the passing of the 1969 Act, and in an age more conscious of the importance of taking children's rights seriously,[240] is thoroughly objectionable and, indeed, unprincipled. And it has led to courts interpreting the 1989 Children Act, which specifically and unequivocally gives a child of sufficient understanding to make an informed decision the right to refuse to submit to a medical or psychiatric examination or other assessment, as nevertheless allowing a child's decision to be overruled.[241]

Conclusion

If a consistent image of children, childhood and welfare does not emerge from cases decided under the three statutes this is at least in part because the statutes themselves do not convey one. There are even inconsistencies within Acts. There is a feeling at times that the legislature may have moved too fast for the judiciary. Certainly the judges seen happier to emphasize the protective function of welfare than to further children's autonomy. On the whole the judicial understanding is intuitive and experiential rather than based on scientific data. The appeal is to the 'common sense' rather than to psychology. Rarely, despite the plethora of material, are the judges looking outside the four corners of the statutes. There are surprisingly few references to the United Nations Convention on the Rights of the Child. Despite *Pepper v Hart*,[242] the use made of extrinsic material is parsimonious. The experiences of other countries, potentially of great value particularly but not exclusively in the area of child abduction, seems to pass the courts by. Above all else one is struck by a shallow understanding of children, childhood and children's rights. This is striking where there are other interests at stake (parents, the medical profession, the integrity of the court process in other countries, security) but is apparent throughout. We are prepared to train our judges in the intricacies of new children's legislation – the experiences with the Children Act 1989 showed this to good effect – but we need to go further. The judiciary of the future needs more critical insight into children's issues. Training can only be part of this process, but it is unquestionably a pre-requisite.

Notes

1   The Short report on Children in Care H.C. 360–361, the DHSS Review of Child Care Law, the White Paper 'The Law on Child Care and Family Services' Cm. 62 (1987), the Law Commission report on Guardianship and Custody (Law Com 172) as well as the Cleveland report Cm. 412 (1988). Decisions of the European Court and the House of Lords' decision in *Gillick v West Norfolk A.H.A.* [1986] AC112 were also formative influences.

2   The Hague Convention and the European Convention.

3   The Latey report (1987) Cmnd. 3342.

4   *The Children Act 1989 Guidance and Regulations*, vols 1–9 (London: HMSO, 1991).

5   *An Introduction To The Children Act 1989* (London: HMSO, 1989).

6   As to which see Michael Freeman, 'In the Child's Best Interest?', (1992) 45 *Current Legal Problems* 173.

7   There were 24 ratifications and 17 accessions as of the end of February 1995.

8   An introduction is Carol S. Bruch, 'International Child Abduction Cases: Experience Under the 1980 Hague Convention' in J. Eekelaar and P. Sarcevic (eds), *Parenthood in Modern Society* (Dordrecht: Nijhoff, 1993), p. 353.

9   There is no satisfactory definition of this in English Law but see the New Zealand case of *Walker v Walker and Harrison* [1981] NZ Recent Law 257 cited by the Law Commission in its Working Paper No. 96, Custody (1985), para. 6.10.

10   [1993] A C 593.

11   On childhood as a social construct see C. Jenks, *Childhood* (London: Routledge, 1996). See also J. Qvortrup, 'Childhood Matters' in J. Qvortrup, M. Bardy, G. Sgritta and H. Wintersberger (eds), *Childhood Matters: Social Theory, Practice and Politics* (Aldershot: Avebury, 1994).

12   To use the language of Karl Llewellyn (see 'My Philosophy of Law' extracted in Lloyd, *Introduction to Jurisprudence* (London: Sweet and Maxwell, 1994), p. 703.

13   *Re A* [1992] 2 All ER 872, 880.

14   *Re B* [1993] 2 FCR 241.

15   *Re B* [1993] FLR 543.

16   Sir Thomas Bingham.

17   In the language of Dame Elizabeth Butler-Sloss in the Cleveland report.

18   *Re S* [1993] 2 FLR 437, 448.

19   As the author of the Cleveland report of 1988.

20   *Re W* [1992] 3 FCR 461, 465.

21   *Re B* [1992] 3 All ER 867, 871.

22   On the meaning of which see *Re A* [1992] Fam 182, 191.

23   See Children Act 1989 s. 1(1).

24   In section 1(3).

25   See *J v C* [1970] A C 668, 770–711. See also *Re K D* [1988] A C 806.

26   See *Re G* [1994] 1 FLR 504, 507–508 and *Re E* [1995] 1 FLR 392, 397. See also David Hershman [1994] 24 Fam. Law 650.

27   *Re M* [1995] 1 FLR 418.

28   *Re A* [1992] Fam 182, 191. See also *Re SC* [1994] 1 FLR 96 and *Re C* [1995] 1 FLR 927 (a similar position obtains in respect of children seeking leave). But cf *Re C* [1994] 1 FLR 26.

29   *Gibson v Austin* [1992] 2 FLR 437 and *Re M* [1994] 1 FLR 760, following the House of Lords decision pre-Children Act of *Richards v Richards* [1984] AC 174.

30   *Re G* [1994] 1 FLR 504 and *Re E* [1995] 1 FLR 392.

31   In *Re G* [1994] 1 FLR 504 at pp. 507–508, and *Re E* [1995] 1 FLR 392, at p. 397 respectively.

32   In *Re G* [1994] 1 FLR 504 at p. 508.

33   It is proposed that a child's welfare should become the paramount consideration in adoption too. This is expected in legislation promised for 1996. On the current position see *Re B* [1995] 1 FLR 895.

34   In the Adoption Act 1976 s.6 it is the first consideration. On the meaning (in the context of surrogacy) see *Re M W* [1995] 2 FLR 759.

35   Human Fertilisation and Embryology Act 1990 s.30.

36   Applications for leave to seek a s.8 order, ouster applications and applications for a secure accommodation order.

37   In *Re M* [1995] 1 FLR 418.

38   See s.25 of Children Act 1989.

39   Op. cit., note 37, pp. 423–424.

40   Ibid., p. 424.

41   *Idem.*

42   *Idem.*

43   *Hereford and Worcester C.C. v S* [1993] 2 FLR 360.

44   Booth J. in *Re W* [1993] 1 FLR 692, and Stuart-White J. in *M v Birmingham City Council* [1994] 2 FLR 141.

45   *Current Law Statutes Annotated, Children Act 1989* (London: Sweet and Maxwell, 1989).

46   *Children: The New Law* (Bristol: Family Law, 1990).

47   *A Guide To The Children Act 1989* (London: Butterworths, 1990).

48   *Children, Their Families and The Law* (Basingstoke: Macmillan, 1992).

49   Volume 1, *Court Orders*, at para. 5.7.

50   *Re A* [1992] Fam 182, 191.

51   [1995] 1 FLR 418.

52   See s. 19(9) (c).

53   *G v Kirklees MBC* [1993] 1 FLR 805. Not that this means that the substantive application is bound to succeed *(C v Salford City Council* [1994] 2 FLR 926).

54   See section 10(9) (where the applicant 'is not the child concerned').

55   See section 10(8); and see *Re S* [1993] Fam 263.

56   *Re S C* [1994] 1 FLR 96 and *Re C* [1995] 1 FLR 927.

57   *Re C* [1994] 1 FLR 26.

58   See White, Carr and Lowe, *The Children Act In Practice* (London: Butterworths, 1995), para. 5.88 and Mary Hayes and Catherine Williams, *Family Law: Principles, Policy and Practice* (London: Butterworths, 1995), pp. 81–82.

59   Per White, Carr and Lowe, op. cit., ante 58, para, 5.88.

60   See Lorraine Fox Harding, 'The Children Act 1989 in Context: Four Perspectives in Child Care Law and Policy' (1991), *Journal of Social Welfare and Family Law* 179–93, 285–302.

61   The child's welfare is the 'golden thread' in wardship: see Dunn J. in *Re D* [1977] Fam 158.

62 *Gibson v Austin* [1992] 2 FLR 437.
63 [1984] A C 174.
64 It held that the criteria in s. 1(3) of the Matrimonial Homes Act 1983 should govern. Children are only one consideration.
65 Op. cit., note 62, p. 441.
66 Ibid., p. 443.
67 *Re G* [1994] 1 FLR 504.
68 Ibid., p. 508 per Balcombe L.J.
69 In particular *Re M* [1995] 1 FLR 418.
70 Ibid., p. 424.
71 *Re A* [1992] Fam 182; *Re SC* [1994] 1 FLR 96; *Re C* [1994] 1 FLR 26; *Re C* [1995] 1 FLR 927.
72 Cf Harold Laski's famous criticism of Kelsen's jurisprudence in *The Grammar of Politics* (4th ed., p. *vi*) (quoted in Lloyd, op. cit., note 12, p. 290).
73 See *Gibson v Austin* [1992] 2 FLR 437.
74 *Birmingham City Council v H (No. 3)* [1994] 2 AC 212. See also *F v Leeds City Council* [1994] 2 FLR 60.
75 *Re T and E* [1995] 1 FLR 581.
76 *Review of Child Law: Custody*, Working Paper No. 96.
77 Op. cit., note 74.
78 Under Children Act 1989 s. 34(4).
79 See *Birmingham City Council v H (No. 2)* [1993] 1 FLR 883, 890.
80 Op. cit., note 47, para. 1.6.
81 A principle first established in *M v M* [1973] 2 All E.R. 81.
82 See op. cit., note 79.
83 Ibid., pp. 891–892 (Balcombe L.J.); p. 899 (Evans L.J.).
84 Ibid., p. 890.
85 *Idem.*
86 Ibid., p. 899.
87 Op. cit., note 74.
88 Ibid., p. 223 per Lord Slynn of Hadley.
89 See Gillian Douglas, 'In Whose Best Interests?' (1994) 110 LQR 379.
90 [1994] 1 FLR 581.
91 Ibid., p. 63.
92 [1995] 1 FLR 581.
93 Ibid., p. 587.
94 Adoption Act 1976 s. 6.
95 Op. cit., note 92, p. 589.
96 In its report on Guardianship and Custody, Law Commission No. 172, para.
97 He cited the reference to it by Wilson J. in *Re F* [1995] 1 FLR 510, 513–514 (see op. cit., note 92, p. 586).
98 Ibid., p. 588.
99 *Nottinghamshire C.C. v P* [1994] Fam 18.
100 And see *Child Protection: Messages From Research* (London: HMSO, 1995).
101 See section 31(2). And see M.D.A. Freeman, 'Legislating for Child Abuse: the Children Act and Significant Harm' in A. Levy (ed.), *Refocus on Child Abuse* (London: Hawksmere, 1994), p. 17.
102 See section 100.
103 Op. cit., note 99, p. 26.
104 Made under s. 37 of the Children Act 1989 (and see ibid., p. 26 and p. 39).

105   Op. cit., note 99, p. 39.
106   A new clause 34 was rejected in the House of Commons on 27th October 1989.
107   Op. cit., note 99, p. 37 (see *Hansard*, H.C. vol. 534, col 1314).
108   See [1993] 1 FLR 514, 537 (This does not appear in the *Official Reports*).
109   See section 31(2).
110   [1993] 1 FLR 281.
111   Ibid., p. 289.
112   [1994] 2 FLR 577.
113   Ibid., p. 588.
114   The first instance decision is not reported.
115   [1994] 1 FLR 73.
116   [1994] 2 FLR 577.
117   Ibid., pp. 586–587.
118   Ibid., p. 587.
119   See A. Bainham (1994) 53 CLJ 458; J. Whybrow (1994) 6 JCL 177 and M. Hayes and
       C. Williams, *Family Law* (London: Butterworths, 1995) (with reservations). But cf J.
       Masson (1994) 6 JCL 170.
120   Op. cit., note 116, p. 587.
121   [1996] 1 FLR 80.
122   See for example, *Dunning v United Liverpool Hospitals' Board of Governors* [1973]
       1 WLR 586.
123   [1993] 1 FLR 281.
124   *Davies v Taylor* [1974] AC 207.
125   Ibid., p. 213.
126   [1995] 1 FLR 643.
127   Op. cit., note 121, p. 95.
128   He was the father of the two youngest girls: the step-father of the two oldest.
129   Op. cit., note 121, p. 94.
130   Of Kennedy L.J.
131   Lord Browne-Wilkinson and Lord Lloyd of Berwick.
132   Op. cit., note 121, p. 102.
133   Ibid., p. 96.
134   On which Felicity Kaganas, Michael King and Christine Piper, *Legislating for Har-
       mony: Partnership Under The Children Act 1989* (London: Jessica Kingsley, 1995).
       See also D. Braun, 'Working with Parents' in Gillian Pugh (ed.), *Contemporary
       Issues In The Early Years: Working Collaboratively For Children* (London: National
       Children's Bureau, 1992). Theoretical insights are offered by Sharon McCallum and
       Isaac Prilletensky, 'Empowerment In Child Protection Work: Values, Practice and
       Caveats', (1996) 10 *Children and Society* 40.
135   See Mary Ann Mason, *From Father's Property to Children's Rights* (New York:
       Columbia University Press, 1994).
136   See *Re A* [1992] Fam 182.
137   Children Act 1989 s.1 (1).
138   [1995] 1 FLR 107.
139   She had removed the children by deceit.
140   Op. cit., note 138, p. 112 (per Thorpe J.).
141   Ibid., p. 113.
142   Ibid., p. 114. See also *Re K* [1995] 1 FLR 977.
143   *R v R* [1995] 2 FLR 625.
144   See *Re N* [1993] 2 FLR 124, 131 (per Balcombe L.J.).

145 See Article 3.
146 On which see *Re J* [1990] 2 AC 562, where the removal from Western Australia was held not to be unlawful because the unmarried father by the law of that country did not have rights of custody.
147 *Re H and Re S* [1991] 3 All ER 230.
148 Ibid., p. 240, per Lord Brandon.
149 [1989] 1 FLR 403.
150 Under Article 5 of the Convention.
151 [1992] 1 FLR 163.
152 Ibid., p. 169.
153 Article 4.
154 See *Re J* [1990] 2 AC 562.
155 [1991] 1 FLR 266.
156 [1992] 1 FLR 548.
157 Ibid., p. 555.
158 [1992] 1 FCR 541.
159 *Re J* [1990] 1 FCR 541.
160 Per Balcombe L.J. in *Re M, The Times*, 3 January 1996.
161 In *Re M*, ibid.
162 *Re V* [1995] 2 FLR 992.
163 In *Re V*, the court rejected the claim that the London home was merely investment property: the mother and child lived there in the winter months.
164 Per Wall J. in *Re W* [1995] 1 FLR 878, 889.
165 *Re W* [1995] 1 FLR 878, 888.
166 [1995] 2 FLR 211.
167 And see also *Re S* [1995] 1 FLR 314, 325: cf *Hallam v Hallam* [1993] 1 FLR 958.
168 [1992] Fam 106.
169 Ibid., p. 119.
170 *Re AZ* [1993] 1 FLR 682.
171 Ibid., p. 691.
172 *Idem.*
173 *Idem.*
174 *Idem.*
175 [1994] 1 FLR 819.
176 Ibid., p. 831 (per Waite L.J.).
177 *Idem.*
178 *Idem.*
179 *Re R* [1995] 1 FLR 716.
180 Ibid., p. 727.
181 Per Wall J. in *Re K* [1995] 1 FLR 977, 986.
182 Article 13 (b).
183 *Re F* [1995] 2 FLR 31.
184 [1991] 1 FLR 413.
185 Ibid., p. 419. See also *Re C* [1989] 1 FLR 403.
186 [1992] 1 FLR 155.
187 Ibid., p. 161.
188 [1995] 1 FLR 64.
189 *Re M* [1995] 1 FLR 1021.
190 *N v N* [1995] 1 FLR 107 (and see above).
191 [1989] 1 FLR 403.

192   [1989] 1 FLR 401.
193   Ibid., p. 405.
194   For example, *Re C (MA)* [1966] 1 All ER 838, the so-called 'blood-tie adoption' case.
195   [1995] 2 FLR 31.
196   See also *Re M* [1996] 1 FLR 315.
197   Op. cit., note 195, p. 38.
198   [1992] 2 FLR 492.
199   There is 'no chronological threshold' (per Balcombe L.J. in *Re R* [1995] 1 FLR 716, 730).
200   [1995] 1 FLR 716.
201   *B v K* [1993] 1 FCR 382; *P v S* [1992] 2 FLR 492.
202   Per Waite L.J. in *Re S* [1994] 1 FLR 819, 827.
203   See *S v S* [1992] 2 FLR 492.
204   See Balcombe L.J.'s remark in *S v S* [1992] 2 FLR 492, 500, approved by Thorpe J. in *N v N* [1995] 1 FLR 107, 112.
205   *Re R* [1992] 1 FLR 105, 107–108.
206   *Re M*, 25 July 1990. Now reported in [1992] 2 FCR 608.
207   [1992] 2 FLR 492, 499.
208   See *Re K* [1995] 1 FLR 977. This statement is *obiter*, because it was held that the child had not reached the age and degree of maturity required.
209   *Re K* [1995] 1 FLR 977.
210   Ibid., p. 996.
211   [1992] 2 FLR 492.
212   Ibid., p. 501.
213   *Re F* [1991] 1 FLR 1 and *G v G* [1991] 2 FLR 506.
214   *D v D* [1994] 1 FLR 137.
215   Ibid., p. 144 (per Balcombe L.J.).
216   See *Re S* [1994] 1 FLR 297.
217   *Idem.*
218   *P v P* [1992] 1 FLR 155, 161 (per Waite J.).
219   *Re M* [1995] 1 FLR 89.
220   *On The Age of Majority*, 1967, Cmnd 3342.
221   *Gillick v. West Norfolk and Wisbech A.H.A.* [1986] AC 112.
222   Particularly Article 12.
223   [1993] 1 FLR 1.
224   Ibid., p. 8.
225   [1992] 1 FLR 190.
226   Ibid., p. 199.
227   See for example Brenda Hoggett, *Parents and Children* (London: Sweet and Maxwell, 1981, p. 12): Peter Bromley and Nigel Lowe, *Family Law* (London: Butterworths, 1987, p. 275).
228   See per Lord Denning MR in *Hewer v Bryant* [1970] 1 QB 357, 369.
229   Per Lord Scarman in *Gillick*, op. cit., note 221.
230   [1986] AC 112.
231   Ibid., pp. 188–189.
232   [1992] 1 FLR 190.
233   And, so it was held, not 'Gillick-competent'.
234   [1993] 1 FLR 1.
235   Ibid., p. 9.
236   *Idem.*

237 Op. cit., note 230, pp. 188–189 (the emphasis is mine).

238 Op. cit., note 232, p. 197 (the emphasis is in the judgment).

239 See the 'legal flak-jacket' metaphor employed in *Re W* (see op. cit., note 234, p. 9).

240 See M.D.A. Freeman, 'Taking Children's Rights More Seriously' (1992), 6 *Int. J. of Law and the Family* 52.

241 *South Glamorgan County Council v W and B* [1993] 1 FLR 574.

242 [1993] AC 593.

6 Statutory Interpretation of European Community Law by English Courts

Margot Horspool

Statutory Interpretation

The European Community legal system has slowly developed into a system *sui generis*. Because of its civil law origins, it started by using the procedures and methods of the civil law systems to interpret Community law, consisting initially of treaty Articles and secondary legislation. Even before the countries which had common law traditions joined the Community (the UK and Ireland in 1973), the European Court of Justice started to develop a body of case law. Although there is no formal system of precedent in the European Community legal system, the practice of the use of *jurisprudence constante*, or consistent case law, gradually grew. Although it is not bound by its previous decisions, the European Court will, therefore, rarely reverse them. On the few occasions when it does so, the event will often have been heralded by one or more Advocate-General's opinions.[1] Case law is now occupying an increasingly important place in Community law, but the civil law practice of interpretation of statutes is still of paramount importance.

Statute law is the primary source of law in the civil law system, which is generally code-based and expects its judges to interpret the existing statutory texts, fill the 'gaps' and clear up ambiguities, but not to make law by setting precedent.

Although the European Community treaties show a close affinity to the concepts, style and methods of the civil law, they also bear the hallmarks of their own unique situation. As Bridge pointed out,[2] they are the result of a negotiated compromise. If this applied to the original treaties, negotiated between six countries with a civil law tradition, it applies with greater force to the Treaty on European Union (TEU), concluded in 1992, which came into force in November 1993, and which was the result of negotiations between 12 member states with different civil law and common law traditions. We should also note that this treaty was drawn up in nine official languages (as against four for the original treaties), and the text resulting from the 1996 Intergovernmental Conference will be drawn up in 11 official languages, the number of member states having risen to 15.

This reinforces the need for such treaties to be couched in more general language than is the case for an English statute, omitting detail and avoiding the complex language of such statutes, but sacrificing the 'greater certainty which a detailed legislative application of the principles would provide'.[3]

As we shall see,[4] the same features are to be found in Community secondary legislation. At first, early directives were often drafted in fairly great detail, trying to achieve as much harmonization as possible between member states. With the so-called 'New Approach' directives, this method has been abandoned and more is now left up to the individual member states to implement this legislation.[5] The growing use of the principle of subsidiarity, newly enshrined in the EC Treaty by the TEU,[6] is also evidence of this same approach.

Methods of Interpretation[7]

If we look at the various types of statutory interpretation as practised by European courts (throughout I shall refer to Europe in its proper geographical sense, that is including the United Kingdom and Ireland), we see that the same methods are known in civil law and in common law jurisdictions, but that the difference lies in the importance attributed to the different methods by the two jurisdictions.

The literal rule   is the traditional common law approach to interpretation. Statute law, although now by far outweighing case law in volume and possibly in importance, has always been regarded as an inferior source of law.[8] The courts have, therefore, interpreted statute law restrictively and prefer the literal meaning of the words. Nevertheless, this rule is contrasted by the golden rule: it is permissible to depart from the clear meaning of a statute if otherwise the result would be absurd or impractical. The mischief rule, as set out in *Heydon's case*,[9] states that the judge must construe statute so as to promote its underlying aim, namely the avoidance of a particular mischief with which the general common law did not deal.

In civil law systems, literal interpretation has its place, albeit a subordinate one. In codified systems it is necessary to rely more heavily on other methods. This also applies to interpretation by the European Court of Justice (ECJ).

The historical approach   common in French law in particular, looks at the *travaux préparatoires*. It is widely used by French judges with the objective of finding the intention of the lawmaker, mostly in recent statutes.[10] It is of less importance in Community law. Very little information exists or is readily accessible about the treaties themselves. There is enough information available concerning the legislative history of secondary legislation, both in Commission documents[11] and in the Official Journal of the European Communities, which publishes proposed legislation in its C-series. The method is, however, used relatively rarely by the ECJ.[12]

In English law, the use of this method was unacceptable until recently. Lord Denning's attempt at 'gap-filling', in *Magor & St. Mellons' RDC v Newport Corp.*[13] was sharply criticized in the House of Lords, when Lord Simonds said:

> It appears to me to be a naked usurpation of the legislative function under the thin disguise of interpretation. And it is the less justifiable when it is guesswork with what material the legislature would, if it had discovered the gap, have filled it in.[14]

However, with the advent of Community law and other methods of interpretation, the rule that no reference at all should be made to Parliamentary records (*Hansard*) has been relaxed. Although cases with a 'European' content had been interpreted by the use of other methods for some time, including reference to *Hansard*,[15] it was perhaps not surprisingly in an English tax case that the House of Lords first allowed reference to parliamentary material. In *Pepper (Inspector of Taxes) v Hart*[16] the Lord Chancellor said:

> If reference to parliamentary material is permitted as an aid to the construction of legislation which is ambiguous, or obscure or the literal meaning of which leads to absurdity, I believe as I have said that in practically every case it will be incumbent on those preparing the argument to examine the whole proceedings on the Bill in question in both Houses of Parliament.

A Practice Note[17] sets the limits to the use of such materials.[18] This states:

> Any party intending to refer to any extract from *Hansard* in support of any such argument as is permitted by the decisions in *Pepper (Inspector of Taxes) v Hart* [1993], 1 All E.R. 42, [1993] AC 593 and *Pickstone v Freemans plc* (1988) 2 All E.R. 203 [1989] AC 66 or otherwise must, unless the judge otherwise directs, serve upon all other parties and the court copies of any such extract together with a brief summary of the argument intended to be based upon such extract.

Comparative interpretation   is used a great deal by the ECJ.[19] Whilst emphasizing the need for its own interpretation of Community law to prevail, the Court regularly looks at the domestic law not only of the country involved in the case, but also of others. In Case 44/79 *Hauer v Land Rheinland-Pfalz*,[20] a case about fundamental rights, the Court said:

> the question of a possible infringement of fundamental rights, by a measure of Community institutions can only be judged in the light of Community law itself. The introduction of special criteria for assessment stemming from the legislation or constitutional law of a particular Member State would, by damaging the substantive unity and efficacy of Community law, lead inevitably to the destruction of the unity of the Common Market and the jeopardizing of the cohesion of the Community.

However, it went on to say:

> that fundamental rights form an integral part of the general principles of the law, the observance of which it ensures; that in safeguarding those rights, the Court is bound to draw inspiration from constitutional traditions common to the Member States.

In case 155/79, *A.M.&S. Europe Ltd v Commission*[21] which concerned the principle of the protection of the lawyer-client relationship, the Court said:

> Community law, which derives from not only the economic but also the legal interpenetration of the Member States, must take into account the principles and concepts common to the laws of those States concerning the observance of confidentiality.

The comparative method is, of course, also used by English courts. The use of comparative law from other common law jurisdictions, however, is much more frequent than any use of comparative law from civil law jurisdictions. In *Derbyshire County Council v Times Newspapers Ltd,*[22] in which the House of Lords dismissed an appeal against a Court of Appeal decision that a local authority could not be sued for defamation, Lord Keith of Kinkel referred to a number of US judgments upholding the right of freedom of speech against local authorities.[23] The Court of Appeal also adverted to Article 10 of the European Convention on Human Rights and relevant case law of the European Court of Human Rights which deals with the right to and limitations of freedom of expression. Lord Keith of Kinkel concluded, however, that the common law was sufficient to help him reach his decision and that there was no need to rely on the European Convention.

The teleological method of interpretation   that is purposive interpretation in the light of the objectives of the legislation, is used in the vast majority of ECJ cases. The changing and evolving nature of Community law, although the texts themselves may stay the same, makes this method ideally suited to the work of the European Court. Time and again the Court has referred to the 'spirit' and the 'general scheme' of the Treaty and has developed its best-known doctrines such as those of direct effect and supremacy of Community law based on this type of interpretation.[24]

The English courts have been using this method of interpretation increasingly with regard to the Community elements in the case law. Lord Denning's guidelines in *Bulmer v Bollinger*,[25] as to whether a case should be referred to the ECJ, and his dictum in that case referring to the incoming tide of Community law, are well-known. He said in *James Buchanan & Co. v Babco Forwarding & Shipping (UK) Ltd*:

> It would be absurd that the Courts of England should interpret it differently from the courts of France, or Holland, or Germany ... We must, therefore, put on one side our traditional rules of interpretation. We have for years tended to stick too closely to the letter – to the literal interpretation of the words. We ought, in interpreting this convention, to adopt the European method ... They adopt a method which they call in English by strange words – at any case they were strange to me – the 'schematic and teleological method of interpretation'. It is not really so alarming as it sounds. All it means is that the judges do not go by the literal meaning of the words or by the grammatical structure of the sentence. They go by the design or the purpose which lies behind ... They then interpret the legislation so as to produce the desired effect. This means that they fill in gaps, quite unashamedly, without hesitation. They ask simply: what is the sensible way of dealing with this situation so as to give effect to the presumed purpose of the legislation? They lay down the law accordingly ... In interpreting the Treaty of Rome (which is part of our law) we must certainly adopt the new approach. Just as in Rome, you should do as Rome does. So in the European Community, you should do as the European Court does.[26]

It has been argued[27] that the teleological approach carries more risk in a municipal law context than in a European one, where it is inevitable because of the imprecise nature of the texts to be interpreted (treaties and so on), the absence of *travaux préparatoires* at least in primary Community law though not in directives and regulations, and the linguistic difficulties with a large number of authentic versions of the same text. The English courts have applied this interpretation to a vast volume of case law, to varying degrees and with varying results.

How do the English Courts Interpret Community Law?

Methods of interpretation are applied differently in the common law and civil law systems. There are even substantial differences between civil law jurisdictions. How, then, can the European Court's avowed intention of obtaining as far as possible a uniform interpretation of Community law in the national courts be achieved?

By taking just a few aspects of Community law which have given rise to the use of 'communautaire' interpretations in the English courts, we can demonstrate the varying degrees of success which the English courts have achieved in dealing with cases with a Community element.

When Should a National Court Refer?

Article 177 of the EC Treaty (as amended by the Treaty on European Union) states:

> The Court of Justice shall have jurisdiction to give preliminary rulings concerning
> (a)   the interpretation of this Treaty;
> (b)   the validity and interpretation of acts of the institutions of the Community and of the ECB;
> (c)   the interpretation of the statutes of bodies established by an act of the Council, where those statutes so provide.
>
> Where such a question is raised before any court or tribunal of a Member State, that court or tribunal may, if it considers that a decision on the question is necessary to enable it to give judgment, request the Court of Justice to give a ruling thereon.
>
> Where any such question is raised in a case pending before a court or tribunal of a Member State against whose decisions there is no judicial remedy under national law, that court or tribunal shall bring the matter before the Court of Justice.

Under Art. 177(2) courts should generally refer questions of interpretation of Community law to the ECJ if this is necessary to come to a decision. Lower courts may refer, but Art. 177(3) provides that courts of last resort must. What, therefore, is a court of last resort?

Art 177(2) provides that 'where such a question is raised before any court or tribunal of a Member State, that court or tribunal may, *if it considers* that a decision on the question is *necessary to enable it to give judgment* request the Court of Justice to give a ruling thereon.' The national court, therefore, must consider that a decision on the question is necessary to enable it to give judgment. It follows that a national court may equally decide that the point of European law is not relevant to its decision, so that it is entitled not to make a reference.

Questions as to whether a decision is necessary and whether the court has a duty to refer[28] were considered recently in two cases: *Chiron Corp. v Murex Diagnostics Ltd*[29] and *R v International Stock Exchange of the UK and the Republic of Ireland, ex p. Else (1982) Ltd.*[30] In *Chiron v Murex* proceedings for infringement of a patent, a High Court Judge struck out certain paragraphs of the defendant's defence and refused leave to add others. There was an unsuccessful appeal to the Court of Appeal, after which the defendant requested the CA to refer certain questions to the ECJ for interpretation and applied for leave to appeal to the House of Lords. Leave to appeal was refused and the request for a reference was adjourned until the time for petitioning the House of Lords for leave to appeal had expired, or until after the petition had been made and refused. After the petition had been refused by the House of Lords the application for a reference to the ECJ was renewed.

Balcombe L.J., giving judgment, pointed out in *Magnavision (SA) v General Optical Council (No. 2)*[31] that, once a domestic court has given judgment and its order has been drawn up, it is *functus officio* and has no power to make a reference under 177. 'This is so both as a matter of domestic law and as a matter of European law.' Staughton L.J., giving a concurring judgment, considered, however, that, although this is undoubtedly true in domestic law, it 'must yield to European law if there is a conflict' (at p.96c). 'If an English court is by European law obliged to make a reference it is no answer that by our domestic law its powers are exhausted.'

The defendant's draft question to be referred to the ECJ was formulated as follows:

> Where the English Court of Appeal has decided a point of EEC law, and the House of Lords refuses leave to appeal to the House of Lords in relation to such point, is it the Court of Appeal or the House of Lords which is subject to the provisions of Article 177 (3) of the Treaty?

It remains without an answer.

From the 'European' point of view, perhaps the Community point, whether it is decisive to the outcome, or might become so, should be referred first to the ECJ. It would be in the spirit of Art. 177(3) to regard that court as a court of last resort from whose decisions no appeal lies as of right. From a practical point of view, however, this would incur extra delay, and the lower court may feel it should first decide the facts, which might then make a reference unnecessary.

In *R v International Stock Exchange of the UK and the Republic of Ireland ex p. Else (1982) Ltd*,[32] the Stock Exchange had suspended the listing of Else (1982) Ltd in June 1989 and subsequently its quotations panel cancelled the listing. The company then appealed to the Quotations Committee which turned down the appeal. The company applied for a judicial review of this decision which was also turned down. During the hearing, one of the questions which arose was whether as shareholders the applicants were entitled under Article 15(1) of Council Directive (EEC) 79/279 (the admission directive) to be notified of, and given the opportunity to make representations about, the committee's impending decision as to whether the company's listing should be cancelled. Article 15 was promulgated with the purpose of co-ordinating the conditions of the admission of securities to official listing in Member States and Article 15(1) provided: 'Member States shall ensure decisions of the competent authorities refusing the admission of a security to official listing or discontinuing such a listing shall be subject to the right to apply to the courts.' It was common ground that the Council of the Stock Exchange had been designated as the competent authority for listing in the UK. The judge directed that a reference be made to the ECJ under Article 177 EEC on the interpretation of Article 15. The Stock Exchange appealed against the judge's direction for a reference.

> Popplewell J. directed that, in order to enable him to give judgment on the application to challenge the panel's decision, two questions on interpretation and effect of the directive be referred to the ECJ:
>
> 1)   Whether Article 15 of the directive was to be interpreted as giving to a registered shareholder in an officially listed company, the listing of which the competent authorities had decided to discontinue, the right to apply to the relevant national court in relation to such decision and
> 2)   whether, where the competent authorities of a member state were considering whether to discontinue the official listing of a company, article 15 conferred a right on a registered shareholder in the company to be heard by the competent authorities in relation to such a decision.

Article 15 of the Directive reads as follows:

> 1.   Member States shall ensure decisions of the competent authorities refusing the admission of a security for official listing or discontinuing such a listing shall be subject to the right to apply to the courts.
> 2.   An applicant shall be notified of a decision regarding his application for admission to official listing within six months of the receipt of the application or, ... within six months of the applicant's supplying such information.

The Stock Exchange appealed against this decision to refer. In its view, the Community law issue should be decided in their favour and the reference would simply cause considerable delay in the proceedings. Sir Thomas Bingham MR delivered the main judgment of the Court of Appeal. He did not share the doubts of the judge below as to the effect to be given to the directive and did not, therefore, deem it necessary that a reference be made. The order under art. 177 was quashed and leave to appeal to the House of Lords was refused.

The central issues were:

1   Whether the applicant shareholders were entitled to be notified about the cancellation of the listing.
2   Whether the applicants were entitled to challenge the Committee's decision.

The correct approach of a national court (other than a final court of appeal) was that a reference should be made if the court could not 'with complete confidence resolve the issue itself ... If the national court has any doubt it should ordinarily refer.'[33]

His Lordship examined the relevant articles of the directive in some detail. In doing so, he referred to the proposal from the European Commission, the opinion of the European Parliament and the opinion of the Economic and Social Committee mentioned in the recitals to the directive. He pointed out that the seventh recital to the directive did not have a precursor in its original draft. He considered this recital to be of sufficient interest to quote it verbatim:

> Whereas there should be the possibility of a right to apply to the courts against decisions by the competent national authorities in respect of the application of this Directive, although such right to apply must not be allowed to restrict the discretion of these authorities.

This recital, however, does not refer to any additional parties such as those in the present case on which the right of appeal should be conferred.

The applicants argued essentially that the directive had direct effect. It was intended to protect shareholders such as the applicants and they could be affected by it. They would not be able to resist a potentially damaging cancellation unless they were notified; the seventh recital of the directive did not impose any restriction upon the parties granted a right to apply to the courts. Thus, it would in fact appear that the directive could be relied upon by the applicants and the English court should seek a ruling from the Court of Justice on the correct construction.

The Master of the Rolls begins by saying that the conditions imposed by national authorities on admission to listing are aimed at the protection of investors, including existing and potential future shareholders. The responsibility of the authorities to protect the interests of investors 'must always be their primary concern when exercising their powers'. However, 'the primary purpose of the directive is to co-ordinate the listing practice of competent authorities in the various Member States with a view to establishing a common market in securities and not, in any direct way, to provide additional protection for investors'. It is true that the applicants may suffer loss, but this also applies in other circumstances, suspension or refusal of a listing, which do *not* confer any additional rights of recourse.

He concludes that in spite of the absence of definition of the parties on whom a right to apply to the courts is conferred in the seventh recital and in Art. 15, the right nevertheless must be conferred on a company or an issuer alone. Even the wider right of appeal advocated by the Economic and Social Committee and the European Parliament does not contain any suggestion that the parties concerned should be other than a company or issuer. The conclusion that the article confers rights on shareholders like the applicants is, therefore, rejected. Sir Thomas Bingham MR then referred to arguments of effectiveness which would be impaired if the regulatory authorities could not take swift and decisive action. If the applicants were given standing, the cost would be substantial and the directive would scarcely have 'avoided all reference to the questions: who is to carry out this task? and who is to pay? Spare though the style of Community draftsmanship may be, it would be surprising to find a lacuna as gross as this.'[34]

The applicants had asserted that the directive has direct effect. The directive does not give a further definition of the term 'investors', which would be understandable if the directive did not confer enforceable rights on investors. If it did, it would be very important to know who are included within the class of investors.

'An instrument of such uncertain scope cannot properly be given direct effect.'[35]

The Master of the Rolls did not share the doubts of the judge below about the effect to be given to the directive and did not find it necessary to seek a ruling on the question.

Leggatt L.J., concurring, undertook a traditional literal interpretation of the directive, rejecting counsel's argument that because the directive is intended for the protection of investors it is they who must apply to the court as a *non sequitur*. He therefore concluded that 'the correct application of Community law is so obvious as to leave no scope for reasonable doubt'.

In other words, it is *acte clair*,[36] so that a reference is not necessary.

When applying the CILFIT criteria to these arguments, the case is not as clear as all that. The criteria include the requirement that the point must be equally obvious to the courts of other Member States and the Court of Justice. This should take account of the characteristic features of Community law, of the different language versions and of the contextual and teleological methods of interpretation of the ECJ. There must be some doubt whether the interpretation of the text of the directive is clear, given all these parameters. In particular, given that this is the first time the Court of Appeal has reversed a request for a reference,[37] and given the uncertainty about which court should be regarded as a court of last resort, perhaps the concern for speedy proceedings should not have outweighed the need for a uniform interpretation of an important piece of Community legislation.

Hartley[38] suggests that for example in interlocutory cases the Court could grant an order and make a reference at the same time. In the instant case Sir Thomas Bingham said, however, that if the facts have been found and the Community laws issue is critical to the court's final decision, the appropriate course is ordinarily to refer the issue to the European Court unless the English court can resolve the issue itself with complete confidence.[39] This could point to a greater willingness to refer generally, albeit not in this case.

The decision by the House of Lords in *Freight Transport Association Ltd (FTA) v London Boroughs Transport Committee (LBTC)*[40] raises questions of (a) the proper approach to the interpretation of directives and (b) the duties of a court from which there is no appeal to refer matters of Community law to the Court of Justice.[41] Two European Directives regulating the condition of heavy vehicles were involved: The Brake Directive 71.320 [1971][42] and the Sound Level Directive 70/157 [1970].[43]

The LBTC imposed a night-time ban on heavy lorries entering Central London without a permit. The issue of such a permit was subject to the fitting of a noise suppressor at a cost of about £30. The FTA applied for a judicial review of the ban advancing as one of the main arguments that the requirement to fit noise suppressors violated the Brake Directive. The Court of Appeal found that it did, and would have been prepared to make the same finding for the Sound Level Directive. No other directive mentioned the use of suppressors, nor did they allow for any specific additional measures to be imposed by the Member States. The Community, having taken the necessary measures, had exclusive competence in this field. Therefore, more rigorous provisions could not be imposed under national laws.

The House of Lords, in Lord Templeman's speech, took a differing view. The Brake Directive (and the Sound Level Directive) concerned the *control* of vehicles, imposing technical and safety requirements on vehicles and exhaust systems, but not the sound of air brakes. Thus, the Directives concerned vehicle control and the LBTC rule concerned environmental

protection and traffic regulation. These were not (yet) the subject of comprehensive and exhaustive legislation by the Community. The LBTC condition was, therefore, held to be lawful as it remained outside the scope of
Community law.

It should be noted that these directives were so-called 'old-style' directives which were aimed to be exhaustive and laid down very specific rules.
Their effect could, therefore, be regarded as inhibiting progress or improvement and was recognized as doing so. The major change which took place
in the way directives were drafted took place with the New Approach to
Technical Harmonization.[44] The new approach is one of *minimum harmonization*, laying down broad objectives rather than detailed rules. There still
has to be total harmonization in that all products should conform to the
Community standard but the methods in attaining that standard are left to
the discretion of the Member States. A safeguard procedure, contained in all
first directives, is now enshrined in Article 100 A(5) by the Single European
Act (SEA) (1986). This did not at the time of the Single European Act
include safeguard measures to protect the environment. Denmark, therefore,
adopted a declaration appended to the SEA indicating it would take unilat-
eral action if necessary.

The TEU now enshrines in its Article 130t the following provision:

> The protective measures adopted pursuant to Article 130s shall not prevent any
> Member State from maintaining or introducing more stringent protective meas-
> ures. Such measures must be compatible with this Treaty. They shall be notified
> to the Commission.

On this basis, the House of Lords would have been able to interpret Community law so as to allow the measure. However, the reasoning followed by
Lord Templeman denied that Community law applied at all and developed
arguments on the principle of subsidiarity and shared competence between
the Community and the Member States.

One thing seems to be clear: the refusal of the House of Lords to refer the
question to the ECJ, something it is bound to do under the provision of
Article 177(3), especially in a case where its decision is a reversal of the
decisions of both the High Court and the Court of Appeal, is suspect from a
point of view of Community law. Such reference may not be necessary
under the CILFIT rules[45] which include the *acte clair* doctrine. There is no
obligation to refer where the point has been decided by a previous Court
ruling, where 'the correct application of Community law may be so obvious
as to leave no scope for any reasonable doubt as to the manner in which the
question raised is to be resolved'. This rule is then qualified by a number of
precautions: 'the matter must be equally obvious to the courts of the other

Member States and to the Court of Justice'. However, even without this rule, which would have to take into account the different interpretation techniques of common law and civil law countries and compare different language versions, this point of interpretation of Community Law is far from clear, nor had it already been decided by the ECJ.

Interim Relief in Community Cases

Factortame Ltd. v Secretary of State for Transport (No. 2)[46]   This was a case referred to the European Court of Justice by the House of Lords. It established that a national court must set aside a rule of national law which prevents a directly effective rule of Community law from having full force and effect.[47]

The House of Lords[48] had to determine whether it was appropriate to grant interim relief until such time as a substantive ruling was given by ECJ.

This case is particularly important in the context of acceptance of English courts of the supremacy of EC law. After the European Court had given its ruling on the reference, and the case returned to the House of Lords, Lord Bridge said:[49]

> If the supremacy within the European Community of Community law over national law of Member States was not always inherent in the EEC Treaty it was certainly well established in the jurisprudence of the Court of Justice long before the United Kingdom joined the Community. Thus, whatever limitation of its sovereignty Parliament accepted when it enacted the European Communities Act 1972 was entirely voluntary.

The ECJ did not indicate what criteria should be adopted for deciding whether to grant interim relief as this was a matter for the national courts. The only requisite is that national remedy must not give less protection to rights derived from Community law than they give to rights based on national law. Although interim relief is a discretionary remedy (guidelines were laid down in *American Cyanamid Co. v Ethicon Ltd*[50]), it may be granted provided there is a serious question to be tried and the balance of convenience favours interim relief.

The *American Cyanamid* case concerned commercial proceedings between private parties. Here the House of Lords decided *American Cyanamid* could not be applied without modification. In particular, it was considered the 'serious question' part of the test was inappropriate. Lord Goff said that

> the court should not restrain a public authority by interim injunction from enforcing an apparently authentic law *unless it is satisfied*, having regard to all the circumstances, that the challenge to the validity of the law is, prima facie, so firmly based as to justify so exceptional a course being taken.[51]

The issue as to when an injunction should be granted also arose in the *British Telecom* case. BT were seeking a mandatory injunction to amend the Utilities Supply and Works Contracts Regulations,[52] so as to relieve BT of certain obligations pending reference of a number of questions to the European Court raised in judicial proceedings brought by BT to quash provisions of Schedule 2 to the regulations. These regulations were intended to implement two Council Directives[53] concerning the opening up of procurement to international competition. BT asserted that under Dir. 90/531 it should be entitled to relief from the obligation under certain circumstances but that the regulations had not correctly given effect to that. The judgment to refuse an injunction in this case followed Lord Goff's criteria for the grant of interim relief in *Factortame (No. 2)*.[54] The outcome of the case on the basis of the questions submitted to the ECJ was far from certain. BT's case was strongly arguable but not bound to succeed. It was not 'sensible for a national court to consider in depth a question which, by referring, it declares itself unable to resolve, which the Court of Justice is, for familiar reasons, better placed to resolve and which the national court will never have to resolve'.[55] BT would suffer difficulties if injunctive relief was denied, but its survival was not at stake, as had been the case for the Spanish fishermen in *Factortame*. This injunction would ask for a very unusual order: 'that H.M.T. lay an instrument before Parliament to amend the Regulations in a sense contrary to what H.M.T. contends to be the true sense of the Directive ... This is not an order we would readily make save in the most compelling circumstances which do not exist here!'[56]

This case encompasses the tensions which exist between English courts and the ECJ. On the one hand, there is no question that a reference should be made as there is a probability that national law and Community law are inconsistent. On the other, the 'loss of sovereignty' evidenced in *Factortame (No. 2)* is clearly kept within the bounds outlined by Lord Goff.

The Court recognized[57] that 'it would be open to Parliament to annul the amendment', that is, to legislate contrary to Community law. This brings us back to the long line of case law and the various dicta concerning the relationship between Community law and national law.[58] In *Macarthys Ltd v Smith*[59] Lord Denning said:

> in construing our statute, we are entitled to look to the Treaty as an aid to its construction, but not only as an aid but as an overriding force ... [However] If the time should come when our Parliament deliberately passes an Act with the intention of repudiating the Treaty ... then I should have thought it would be the duty of our courts to follow the statute of our Parliament.

Lord Diplock in *Garland v British Rail Engineering Ltd*[60] cited section 2(4) of the European Communities Act 1972.[61] He confirmed that this was the proper approach to take, but based his reasoning on ordinary English rules of construction of international law.[62]

Recent Case Law before the English Courts

R v Secretary of State for the Home Department Ex parte Flynn[63]   The case concerned Art. 7(a) of the EC Treaty, which provides:

> The Community shall adopt measures with the aim of progressively establishing the internal market over a period expiring on 31 December 1992. The internal market shall comprise an area without internal frontiers in which the free movement of goods, persons, services and capital is ensured in accordance with the provisions of this Treaty.

Lord Justice Leggatt, giving the judgment of the Court, said the appellant had argued that article 7(a) required EC Member States to abolish internal frontier controls by December 31, 1992, and that this requirement had direct effect, that is it could be invoked by an individual against the State[64] or indeed against another individual.[65]

The Court referred to *Hurd v Jones v Inspector of Taxes*[66] where the European Court of Justice repeats the criteria for direct effect, laid down in *Van Gend & Loos*, and says:

> A provision produces direct effect in relations between the Member States and their subjects only if it is clear and unconditional and not contingent on any discretionary measure. *Hurd v Jones* concerned Art. 5 EC which states that Member States shall take all appropriate measures whether general or particular, to ensure fulfilment of the obligations arising out of this Treaty or resulting from actions taken by the institutions of the Community. They shall facilitate the achievement of the Community tasks. They shall abstain from any measure which would jeopardise the attainment of the objectives of this Treaty.

This provision was held by the ECJ to be too vague to have direct effect.
The *Van Gend & Loos* criteria may be summarized as follows:[67]

1   The provision must be clear and unambiguous.
2   It must be unconditional.
3   Its operation must not be dependent on further action being taken by Community or national authorities.[68]

When these criteria were applied by the ECJ to the second *Defrenne* case[69] it held that Article 119 did have direct effect. Article 119 reads:

Each Member State shall during the first stage ensure and subsequently maintain the application of the principle that men and women should receive equal pay for equal work.

There was, therefore, a deadline in this case (the end of the first stage), as there is in the instant case. The ECJ held that[70] the requirement of further action did not prevent Art. 119 from being directly effective after the deadline had passed. In the instant case the Court of Appeal pointed out that it is a requirement for the Community to establish the internal market and that Member States could not carry out such measures without direction from the Community. If the Member States had meant to provide for an obligation to maintain an internal market irrespective of whether the necessary measures to establish an internal market had already been adopted, 'then words would surely have been used to state that intention and that effect'.

In the view of the Court, few, if any, of the Member States had adhered to the abolition of identity controls at internal frontiers and this, although it did not aid the construction of Article 7(a), nevertheless led to the conclusion that no precise obligation had been imposed. This statement may come as a surprise to those who travel regularly throughout the European Union and cross most frontiers (albeit not those of the UK) without undergoing identity checks. The advent of the Schengen Convention, although not a Community instrument, nevertheless had as its intended result precisely the abolition of personal identity checks at frontiers, although at the time of writing the implementation of the Convention has encountered more than one difficulty. The judge concluded that, in view of the many implementing measures necessary and the amount of room left for the exercise of discretionary power, 'broadly though one might construe the article' it was not possible to conclude that the article had direct effect. Counsel's suggestion that Article 7(a) might have direct effect if read in conjunction with Articles 5, 6 or 59 also failed.

There is no mention of an Article 177 reference to the ECJ for interpretation of the article. It may be that leave to appeal to the House of Lords will be granted and that a reference will still be made. However, in view of the difficulties described above as to what 'a court against whose decisions there is no appeal' means, it surely would have been right to refer this case. The CILFIT rules do not apply here, there is no *acte clair* and an interpretation by the ECJ as to the direct effect or absence thereof of Article 7(a) would have been helpful.

R v Secretary of State for the Home Department, Ex parte Vitale e Do Amaral[71]   This case before the Queen's Bench Divisional Court concerned two EU citizens resident in the UK who had received income support while seeking work. As they were now no longer looking for work, they received letters from the Home Department informing them that they would no longer receive income support. They applied for judicial review of this decision. Judge J. interpreted Article 8a of the EC Treaty, inserted by the TEU, in conjunction with Article 48EC. Article 48 provides that those in search of employment may freely move within the territory of the EU. This right also includes the right to receive income support.[72]

Article 8a provides:

> (1) Every citizen of the Union shall have the right to move and reside freely within the territory of the Member States, subject to the limitations and conditions laid down in this Treaty and the measures adopted to give it effect.

Article 8e provides for the adoption of further provisions to strengthen or add to the rights laid down in the article.

The rights to reside and move freely are, therefore, not absolute: they are 'expressly and unequivocally subject to the limitations and conditions contained in the EC treaty'. This included the provisions under Article 48, which, in the opinion of the judge, were not rendered nugatory. Continuing his 'communautaire' interpretation, the judge referred not only to Council directives and case law of the European Court, but also to Commission reports and academic writings. As the applicants had ceased to be economically active, they were no longer exercising Community rights and their presence ceased to be lawful. Consequently, they were no longer entitled to income support. Deportation was not in issue as that would create a prohibition on their re-entering the UK, which would clearly be in conflict with Community law.

Having reached a clear conclusion his Lordship 'resisted the temptation to refer the question to the European Court for its consideration'.

It would appear that more recently, perhaps under the influence of the principle of subsidiarity,[73] the courts have been more and more inclined to carry out their own interpretation of Community law. Although this development has been encouraged by the ECJ generally, overburdened by an increase in the number of cases, in its CILFIT judgment and in its interpretation of *acte clair,* and must surely be welcomed, a reference in this last case could well have clarified the status and meaning of Art. 8a, including the question of whether it might have direct effect.

Whatever one may think of the interpretation used in any of the cases described, they demonstrate how difficult the goal of uniform application of Community law is to attain.

Notes

1   See for example Case C–10–89, *SA SNL–Sucal NV v Hag GF AG*, [1990] ECR I–3711, following Advocate–General Jacobs' Opinion and Cases C–267 & 268/91, *Keck & Mithouard, Criminal Proceedings against*, [1993] ECR I–6097, but see Case 91/92, *Faccini Dori v Recreb Srl*, [1995] All ER (EC) 1, where the ECJ did not follow AG Lenz's opinion to reverse its previous case law.

2   Bridge, 'National Legal Tradition and Community Law; Legislative Drafting and Judicial Interpretation in England and the European Community', *JCMS*, XIX (4) June 1981, p. 351.

3   *The Preparation of Legislation*, Cmnd. 6503 (1975), p. 55.

4   *Freight Transport Association Ltd v London Boroughs Transport Committee* [1991] 3 All ER 915.

5   Art. 189(3) EC: 'A directive shall be binding, as to the result to be achieved, upon each Member State to which it is addressed, but shall leave to the national authorities the choice of form and methods.'

6   Article 3b EC, as amended by the TEU:

>   The Community shall act within the limits of the powers conferred upon it by the Treaty and the objectives assigned to it therein.
>
>   In areas which do not fall within its exclusive competence, the Community shall take action, in accordance with the principle of subsidiarity, only if and in so far as the objectives of the proposed action cannot be sufficiently achieved by the Member States and can, therefore, by reason of the scale or effects of the proposed action, be better achieved by the Community.
>
>   Any action by the Community shall not go beyond what is necessary to achieve the objectives of this Treaty.

7   See also: V. Sacks and C. Harlow, 'Interpretation, European Style', (1977) MLR 40, p. 578.

8   See C. Ilbert, *Legislative Methods and Forms* (Clarendon Press Oxford, 1909), p. 1.

9   3 Co. Rep. 7a, 76 Eng. Rep. 637.

10   See MacCormick and Summers, *Interpreting Statutes, A Comparative Study*, (1991) Dartmouth, Aldershot, Ch. 6 at p. 186.

11   For example the EU Bulletins.

12   For example Case 29/69, *Stauder v City of Ulm*, [1969] ECR 419.

13   [1952] AC 189, 191.

14   *Magor & St. Mellon's RDC v Newport Corp.* [1952] AC 189, 191.

15   In *Pickstone v Freemans plc* [1988] 2 All ER 203, [1989] AC 66.

16   [1993] All ER 42, 47.

17   [1995] 1 All ER 234.

18   See Bennion's Comments in *All ER Annual Review* 1992, p. 381, which does not refer to any 'foreign' methods of interpretation and argues from a strictly orthodox common law view.

19   See Case 29/69 *Stauder v City of Ulm*, [1969] ECR 419, which gives an example of the linguistic difficulties in the interpretation of Community law; Case 11/70 *Internationale Handelsgesellschaft v Einfuhr- und Vorratsstelle für Getreide und Futtermittel*, [1970] ECR 1125, [1972] CMLR 255.

20   [1979] ECR 3727, [1980] 3 CMLR 42.

21   [1982] ECR 1575, [1982] CMLR 264.

22   [1993] 1 All ER 1011.

23 At p. 1018 *City of Chicago v Tribune Co.* [1923] 307 Ill 595; *New York Times Co. v Sullivan* [1964] 376 US 254 at 277.

24 See for example: Case 26/62 *van Gend en Loos v Nederlandse Administratie der Belastingen*, [1963] ECR 1; [1963] CMLR 105: 'To ascertain whether the provisions of an international treaty extend so far in their effects it is necessary to consider the spirit, the general scheme and the wording of the provisions'; Case 14/83 *von Colson & Kamann v Land Nordrhein-Westfalen*, [1984] ECR 1891; [1986] 2 CMLR 430: '26. ...The Member States' obligation arising from a directive to achieve the result envisaged by the directive and their duty under Article 5 of the Treaty to take all appropriate measures, whether general or particular, to ensure the fulfilment of that obligation is binding on all the authorities of the Member States including the courts.'; Case C–106/89, *Marleasing SA v La Comercial Internacional de Alimentacion SA* [1990] ECR I–1435, [1992] 1 CMLR 305, a case concerning a directive which did not have direct effect: '8...the national court called upon to interpret is required to do so, as far as possible, in the light of the wording and the purpose of the directive'.

25 [1974] 2 WLR 202, [1974] 2 CMLR 91.

26 P. 112 (1976) 2 WLR 107, [1977] QB 208, 213–14. Cf *Bulmer v Bollinger S.A.* [1974] 1 Ch. 401, 425.

27 By Sacks and Harlow see n. 7.

28 See discussion on this point in T.C. Hartley, *The Foundations of European Community Law*, (Oxford: Clarendon Press, 1994, 3rd edn.).

29 [1995] All ER (EC) 88.

30 [1993] 1 All ER 420.

31 [1987] 2 CMLR 262 especially at pp. 265–266.

32 CA [1993] 1 All ER 420.

33 At p. 426f.

34 At p. 431a.

35 At p. 431e.

36 See Case 283/81 CILFIT ([1982] ECR 3415 which laid down criteria for circumstances in which a reference is not necessary.

37 In *SA Magnavision v General Optical Council (No. 2)* [1987] 2 CMLR 262 the Queen's Bench Divisional Court refused to refer where the judgment had already been given and leave to appeal had been refused, for reference at this stage could in no sense be interpreted as 'preliminary'.

38 See n. 28 *supra*.

39 At p. 426f.

40 [1991] 3 All ER 915, [1992] 1 CMLR 5.

41 All ER Annual Review 1991 p. 146.

42 [1971] JO L 202/37; Eng.Sp.Ed [1971] OJ 746.

43 JO L 42/16; Eng.Sp.Ed. [1970] OJ 111.

44 [1985] OJ C136/1.

45 Case 283/81, [1982] ECR 3415, [1983] 1 CMLR 472.

46 Case C–213/89 [1991] 1 All ER 70, [1990] ECR I–2433.

47 See All ER Annual Review 1990 p. 102.

48 [1991] All ER 70 at 106.

49 [1991] 1 AC 603, 658.

50 [1975] 1 All ER 504.

51 Ibid., p. 20. See also *R v H.M. Treasury, ex parte British Telecommunications plc* [1994] 1 CMLR 621.

52 SI 1992 No. 3279.

53   Dir. 90/531 EEC and 92/13 EEC, the Remedies Directive.
54   At pp. 672, 673, 674B.
55   At 43, p. 648.
56   At 47, p. 649.
57   At 47.
58   See for an exhaustive discussion of the relevant line of case law: Lawrence Collins, *European Community Law in the United Kingdom* (Butterworths, 1990) 4th edn., and also C. Barnard and R. Greaves, The application of Community law in the United Kingdom 1986–1993, CML Rev, 1994, 31(5), p. 1055.
59   (1979) 3 All ER 325 CA, at p. 329.
60   [1983] 2 AC 751.
61   'Any enactment passed or to be passed, other than the one contained in this Part of this Act, shall be construed and have effect subject to the foregoing provisions of this section'. The 'foregoing provisions' include s. 2(1) which provides that directly enforceable Community law is to be given effect in the UK.
62   [1983] 2 AC 771.
63   CA, Judgment 7 July 1995, *The Times* Law Report 20/7/95.
64   In *Van Gend & Loos, supra.*
65   *Defrenne v Sabena*, case 43/75, [1976] ECR 455.
66   Case 44/84, [1986] 2 CMLR.
67   See A. Dashwood, The Principle of Direct Effect in European Community Law (1978) 16 *Journal of Common Market Studies* 229, at 231 et seq.
68   Hartley, *The Foundations of European Community Law* (Oxford: Clarendon Press, 1994), 3rd edn., p. 200.
69   Case 43/75 [1970] ECR 455.
70   At p. 455.
71   [1996] All ER (EC) 461 CA.
72   See also *R v IAT, ex parte Antonissen*, case C–292/89, [1991] ECR I 745.
73   Art 3b EC.

7   Interpreting Treaties in the United Kingdom

Richard Gardiner

To describe the subject as 'interpreting treaties' somewhat pre-empts a central question when examining statutory interpretation in the context of treaties. For one approach has it that it is the statute, not the treaty, that fails to be interpreted with the treaty itself simply a background aid. That, however, is a distinction which cannot be effectively applied. The background can only aid if it is attributed a meaning.

Thus three matters appear particularly appropriate for investigation when considering statutes which are related to treaties. First, in the relationship between statutes and treaties, there is the diversity of approaches in legislation implementing treaties to which the United Kingdom is, or is about to become, a party. Second, it is necessary to establish in what circumstances a court will look at a treaty and decide whether to interpret it. Third, if courts in the United Kingdom[1] do interpret treaties (as distinct from interpreting just the statutes embodying or in some way connected with them), how do they approach them? Is a distinct process of interpretation adopted for statutes of the type under consideration and are treaties subjected to a different form of interpretation from statutes?

The interpretation of statutes which set out provisions of treaties or in some other way import them into English law is probably the most significant of these subjects for investigation as the two other areas are precursors to interpretation, whether in actual litigation or when prediction of a judicial decision is the determining factor in giving advice. Thus the outcome of actual or predicated litigation on a point involving a treaty may be significantly influenced by factors arising in the first and second areas of inquiry.

The case law on interpretation of treaties is at a stage of development which leaves it difficult to state a single set of applicable rules or principles. This is because of a mismatch between public international law and law in the United Kingdom and because the choice of rules for interpretation has not been firmly made. The underlying notion that public international law is a system of law entirely separate from that in the United Kingdom can be put in question by indications that some rules of public international law are accepted as automatically being part of English law, that is without legislative or judicial intervention to make them such.

The central question considered here is which rules apply in English law for interpreting treaties. Public international law, the legal system under which treaties are drawn up and put into force, now has its own rules of treaty interpretation set out in a code of treaty law. This is the *Vienna Convention on the Law of Treaties*.[2] Though other elements of this code are not universally applicable as rules of public international law, the rules of treaty interpretation (described here as 'the Vienna rules') are.

The judges in English courts, however, show only limited awareness of these rules and make but spasmodic use of some of them. Where such use has been made, virtually no explanation has been given as to how the rules, or some of them, fail to be applied in courts in the United Kingdom. They have not been given statutory force; but as some (particularly those on the preparatory work of a treaty) are invoked in judgments of English courts, what ground is there for not applying the rest? The tendency of the judges, however, is to use an amalgam of established rules of statutory interpretation with some extension to allow reference to the preparatory work of a treaty that is in issue,[3] and with judicial inventiveness in formulating rules that come conveniently to mind.[4]

To understand the present position it is necessary first to be aware of the general relationship between public international law and the law in the United Kingdom; second to identify the different ways in which treaties are taken into account by statute; and third to try to be clear about when the courts may regard themselves as engaging in interpretation of a treaty and how they go about it.

Public International Law Background

At the root of the uncertainties over interpretation of treaties in English law lies the innate reluctance of the British judiciary and legal profession to recognise or accept that public international law is actually law.[5] This is puzzling because the English judicial tradition did not depend on an established and comprehensive legislative structure when rules were being developed and applied as common law.

A reluctance to accept and apply rules of public international law also sits ill with the internationalist approach adopted in some areas, such as maritime law (though perhaps with the emphasis on English law as providing the benchmark for rules of international application), and with the occasional pronouncements of the courts that the 'law of nations' (a synonym for what is now usually described as 'public international law') is part of English law.[6]

Diversity of means of development has been a feature of English law. Legislation has been as much a means of codification and development of the common law as have judicial decisions been a means of developing interpretations of statutes. As already noted, the English judiciary has found little difficulty in creative use of common law, just as at the other end of the scale of significance in relatively recent times British colonial magistrates took readily to the application of local customary law.[7]

In the broadly comparable, if less advanced, process of development of international law, customary rules and, in ever increasing quantities in recent times, treaties have interacted to establish the law. This is particularly well shown in the work of the International Law Commission which has a mandate requiring codification and progressive development of the law, a mandate which the Commission mainly fulfils by drawing up multilateral treaties.

To the above must be added the qualification that a few judges have tried to make sense of the relationship between public international law and English law. Lord Denning in *Trendtex Trading v Bank of Nigeria* said:

> seeing that the rules of international law have changed – and do change – and that the courts have given effect to the changes without any Act of Parliament, it follows to my mind inexorably that the rules of international law, as existing from time to time, do form part of our English law.[8]

The evidence for such acceptance by the courts is, however, scant; and in any event, in the case of a treaty some legislative treatment of the international instrument is virtually a *sine qua non* if the court is to consider the treaty as within the ambit of the law to be applied.

Difficulty with perceptions of the relationship of public international law with English law can be seen in the linguistic confusion in discussion of this subject. In the *Trendtex* case[9] Lord Denning uses 'incorporation' to describe a process by which rules of international law may automatically become part of English law without legislative or judicial intervention, this being distinguished in his terms from 'transformation' which involves legislative or judicial action to bring rules of public international law into English law.

Yet such an analysis of the possible reception of international law in English law as an automatic process (that is without Parliamentary intervention) with the label 'incorporation' is exactly the contrary of the notion of 'incorporation' as used in the context of treaties. In the case of treaties, by well established precept, legislative intervention is the only mode by which the provisions of a treaty may be given effect or brought into English law, such a process being described as 'incorporation'.[10]

Statutory Means for Implementing Treaties

The means by which Parliament gives effect in English law, or enables effect to be given, to treaties also suffers from confusing terminology for identifying or analysing what Parliament does. 'Incorporation' has already been noted as something of a Janus in this context. In a somewhat similar way 'direct' and 'indirect' can be confusingly applied to enactments giving effect to treaties.

The older way in which legislation has been used to implement obligations in a treaty which is to bind the United Kingdom has been for the operative provisions of the treaty to be translated into the form and terminology of provisions in an Act of Parliament. This approach has been described as 'direct' enactment.[11]

Such a method has the advantage that the wording and structure of the law in the treaty are converted into the idiom and order of the United Kingdom, though the method bears the risk of inadvertently departing from the requirements of the treaty. It may also disguise the language of the treaty and could be a strong contributory factor in the preference English judges show for using inappropriate English methods of construction and interpretation when they are addressing provisions derived from a treaty.

A second means of giving effect to treaties by legislation is to state that the provisions of the treaty (or any of them that require implementation in domestic law) are to have effect as law in the United Kingdom, or in specified territory of the United Kingdom. Using this method, the words of the treaty are often reproduced in a Schedule to the Act or, in some cases, in subordinate legislation.[12] This has been described as 'indirect enactment'.[13]

Such analytical descriptions, however, are not used uniformly by lawyers and judges. Whether in fact it would be more apt to describe use in legislation of the actual text of treaty provisions as 'direct' enactment, rather than using a transformed version, may be a question of perspective or preference. Provided the intended use of language is made clear by definition, little harm will follow from use of one term rather than the other.

There is, however, a considerable potential in the differing legislative methods for influencing the approach taken by the judiciary. This is considered in more detail below, but some of the issues which the choice of method may raise can be seen in the statement of Lord Oliver when he said:

Where, for instance, a treaty is directly incorporated into English law by Act of the legislature, its terms become subject to the interpretative jurisdiction of the court in the same way as any other Act of the legislature.[14]

Aside from the uncertainty as to what he meant by '*directly* incorporated',[15] what is also unclear is whether the observation indicates the circumstances in which a court is to construe a treaty, how it is to perform that task and whether there are any considerations to be taken into account different from those applying in other situations of statutory construction.

Other instances of courts referring to treaties when applying statutes either follow from variants of one of the two methods of implementing treaties described above or occur in application of more general principles of statutory interpretation. Thus there have been cases where legislation does not expressly refer to a treaty but it is nevertheless apparent that it does implement or reflect provisions of a treaty. Equally there is the principle of statutory interpretation that where there is legislative ambiguity or uncertainty over a point which could bear on the United Kingdom's international obligations, such ambiguity or uncertainty should be resolved in a manner consistent with those obligations rather than in violation of them.[16]

It may not always be clear whether it is unexpressed implementation of a treaty provision or application of the principle of seeking to conform to international obligations which is informing the judicial approach in a particular case. In *Mandla v Dowell Lee*[17] the House of Lords had to consider the meaning of 'racial' group and 'ethnic origins' in the Race Relations Act 1976. Lord Fraser, while finding it unnecessary to rely on any special rule of construction for legislation giving effect to international conventions, said:

Neither the Race Relations Act of 1976 nor its predecessors in the United Kingdom, the Race Relations Acts of 1965 and 1968, refer to the International Convention on the Elimination of All Forms of Radical Discrimination (1969) (Cmnd. 4108). The Convention was adopted on March 7, 1966, subject to reservations which are not now material. It was not ratified by the United Kingdom until March 7, 1969. Under the Convention the states parties undertook, *inter alia*, to prohibit discrimination in all its forms, and to guarantee the rights of everyone 'without distinction as to race, colour, or national or ethnic origin' of equality before the law, notably in certain rights which were specified including education (article 5(e) (v)). The words which I have quoted are very close to the words found in the Act of 1976 and in its predecessors in this country, and they are certainly quite consistent with these United Kingdom Acts having been passed in implementation of the obligation imposed by the Convention.[18]

What this suggests is that where the British system of legislating to give effect to treaty obligations does not specifically refer to the treaty or use its actual words, the courts may view the international obligations of the United Kingdom as a relevant element but without assuming any responsibility for trying to ensure that an interpretation is reached specifically in the light of those obligations. Such a role may be viewed as properly falling to Parliament, a role which it can fulfil by legislating when there is an issue of treaty interpretation on which the courts may require guidance;[19] or Parliament may set up some continuing process for implementation.[20]

A recent example of the latter can be seen in the Asylum and Immigration Appeals Act 1993. Section 2 states: 'Nothing in the immigration rules (within the meaning of the 1971 [Immigration] Act) shall lay down any practice which would be contrary to the Convention.'[21] Since immigration rules are subject to Parliamentary approval, this means that Parliament has a measure of control over ensuring that the Refugee Convention's obligations are observed. However, the question of whether a practice under the rules is contrary to the Convention may come before the courts in proceedings for judicial review and thus require a court to consider the proper interpretation of the Convention itself.[22]

Consideration of Treaties by the Courts

The attention of a court will generally be drawn to a potentially relevant treaty either by implementing legislation which directly or indirectly[23] leads to the treaty's consideration or because the treaty forms part of the background to the dispute or of the body of law in a general sense pertinent to the dispute. Obviously the terms of the treaty itself may give an indication of whether it purports to cover the matter in hand. To that extent, at the very least, when a court makes its initial decision to investigate whether a treaty is to be taken into account it may be necessary for the court to interpret the treaty.

However, it should be stressed that the decision to look at a treaty and to consider its potential relevance is generally only part of the process of ascertaining the relevant law. In this process a court will reach its own view on the interpretation of the treaty's provisions; but it does not necessarily follow from this that such an interpretation will be authoritative in the sense of binding the parties to the treaty or establishing a precedent for its future interpretation.

In fact, when a court within a state interprets and applies a treaty it is unlikely that it will be ruling on a dispute between states parties to a treaty. In the light of this it is necessary to approach the notion of 'interpretation of a treaty' with some caution. Such a process of interpretation probably does not mean adjudicating on the treaty as between the parties bound by it.

Equally it does not mean ruling on the effect of the treaty as an instrument of international law but rather as an element of law relevant to a matter or dispute governed by municipal law.

In the latter sense it is difficult to see what objection there could be to English courts taking a view on the meaning of a treaty, were the judges equipped with a clear legal policy on which rules of interpretation to use and, if using the Vienna rules, a willingness to apply them as they would be applied in their natural habitat.[24]

One preliminary point falling within the domestic law sphere is whether ambiguity must be found in the statutory provision if a lead to a treaty is to be followed up. One view is that only where the words of the statutory provision are 'reasonably capable of more than one meaning' is the treaty relevant.[25] As to this, the Law Commission has noted:

> This does not seem to deal with the situation where the words of a provision, in the context of the national instrument alone, appear reasonably to have only one meaning, although in the context of a treaty they might offer a choice of meanings.[26]

This problem comes into even sharper focus when the English rules of statutory interpretation point to a clear meaning while application of the Vienna rules to the same words in a treaty would yield differing possible meanings.[27]

That point aside, where there is legislation which gives effect to a treaty, or where there is an implicit connection between a statute and a treaty, courts have no difficulty with the initial hurdle of deciding whether to consider the treaty. It may be more helpful, therefore, simply to consider those cases where courts will not look at a treaty, or will only look at it as background but reject it as part of the applicable law.

This distinction can be seen by comparing the cases of *In Re Westinghouse*[28] and *British Airways v Laker Airways*.[29] The former case concerned the Evidence (Proceedings in Other Jurisdictions) Act 1975. One question was whether a request from a foreign court should be granted for evidence to be taken in the United Kingdom where grounds were advanced for refusing this under a treaty. Though the 1975 Act made no reference to the relevant Hague Convention,[30] the House of Lords accepted that the Act was passed, at least in part, to give effect in English law to the Convention. That implicit tie to the Convention entitled the court to consider whether the particular request was inconsistent with the provisions of the Act in the light of the Convention provisions which it implemented.[31]

In contrast, in *British Airways v Laker Airways*[32] the House of Lords was invited to consider whether a British airline's assertions that other British airlines had violated the law by setting fares which damaged its business should be tried under English law or American law. Procedures for setting fares and regulation of agreements between airlines on fares were the subject of provisions in a treaty, a bilateral air services agreement between the United Kingdom and the USA.

It was well established in English case law that such a treaty is not part of English law[33] even though it, and similar agreements, formed the background to the dispute and contained provisions which were pertinent to the question of whether the policy of English law on the tort of conspiracy and commercial agreements between airlines should prevail over American law. As the air services agreement was not part of English law, even implicitly in the sense of the Hague Convention described above, the House of Lords did not take into account (still less interpret) the provisions of the treaty.[34]

Similarly, in *J.H. Rayner (Mincing Lane) v Dept of Trade and Industry*[35] the treaty establishing the International Tin Council (ITC), the Sixth International Tin Agreement, had not been made part of English law even though it was mentioned in an Order in Council[36] concerning privileges and immunities under the International Organisations Act 1968, an Order which also conferred on the ITC the legal capacities of a body corporate. The issue in the litigation concerned aspects of the personality of the ITC as an international legal person. Though the House of Lords considered the International Tin Agreement as a relevant background fact, the effect of the Agreement as the constitution of the ITC was not before the House. It was not a matter governed by English law.

The conclusion to be drawn is that issues of interpretation of treaty provisions may come before a court as part of the law to be applied to a matter in dispute only where legislation directly or by implication makes the treaty provisions part of the law within the United Kingdom. In other cases a treaty may be part of the relevant background but will not be interpreted by a court as having any dispositive role in the disputed matter.

Interpretation of Treaty Provisions[37]

The conclusion stated above on the circumstances in which courts in the United Kingdom will consider and interpret treaties does not lead to a complete explanation of the position adopted by courts when interpreting provisions originating in treaties. This is because the judges have not formulated any clear rationale for their approach to such provisions as part of the body of English law, or as recognized or received into English law. Further, in their approach to interpreting such provisions lies confusion. For it remains unclear whether the courts consider that they are applying English rules of statutory interpretation to statutory provisions or are using rules of public international law for interpretation of treaties.

Thus there are two questions in this area. First, is a court which refers to a treaty simply using its text as an aid to interpreting a statute rather than interpreting the treaty itself? The significance of this issue as a possible pointer to whether English rules of statutory interpretation are to be applied to the text of the treaty or the rules of public international law furnishes the second question. Are English courts to use the Vienna rules to interpret treaties?

It would, however, be quite possible, even if the treaty were simply viewed as an aid to interpretation of a statute (rather than an external legal instrument whose effect is made law by a statute), to conclude that in order to find the correct meaning of the treaty's provisions the rules of public international law should be applied.

On the first question, the language of judgments in the higher courts in the United Kingdom suggests an approach narrowly centred on the legislation to the exclusion of a broader view of the treaty which may have inspired the legislation.

A prominent example of this is *Hiscox v Outhwaite*.[38] The central issue was where an arbitral award is 'made'. This arose in applying the Arbitration Act 1975 which gave effect to the New York Arbitration Convention of 1958. The Act did not set out provisions of the Convention verbatim but in defining 'Convention award' referred to 'an award made ... in the territory of a State ... party to the New York Convention'.[39] The question was how this applied in the situation where every element of the arbitration was connected with England save that the arbitrator signed the award while in Paris.

The Court of Appeal and House of Lords paid little more than lip service to the undisputed fact that the words were those of the New York Convention. In the House of Lords the judges clearly saw themselves as engaged in interpretation of the Arbitration Acts with the preparatory work of the Convention as a legitimate aid to that task, rather than as an element in interpreting the Convention which lay behind the legislation. In other words, the exercise was not acknowledged as one of treaty interpretation. It was solely one of statutory interpretation. This had the consequences (considered below) that the New York Convention was not interpreted as a treaty would be interpreted applying public international law and that a proper role for the rules on interpretation in the Vienna Convention on the Law of Treaties was thus effectively excluded.

If the House of Lords viewed their task as removed from any real attempt at proper interpretation of the Convention, the Court of Appeal revealed little sign of any systematic approach to interpretation of provisions originating in a treaty. Nevertheless, the source of this confusion may not be just the lack of any conceptual framework for relating statutory provisions to their treaty origins; for it also seems to stem from uncertainty over the rules of public international law for interpretation of treaties (the Vienna rules).

At this point, therefore, the focus slips from the search for a coherent and consistent analysis of the relationship between statutory and treaty provisions to an investigation of the approach taken by courts to interpretation and whether there is any sensible scheme to be found in the use made by the courts of the Vienna rules. Were these rules to be applied consistently and in their entirety, that would provide an answer (at least in the context of interpretation) to whether treaty provisions become ordinary statutory provisions once made the subject of a statute or whether they retain something of their character as creatures of public international law.

In *Fothergill v Monarch Airlines*[40] the House of Lords initiated an unfortunate trend in the use of the Vienna rules by concentrating on only one aspect of them. In that case three of the judges referred to the Vienna rules to support their use of the preparatory work of the relevant treaty when trying to determine whether 'damage' included partial loss of contents of a suitcase slit open during performance of a contract for carriage by air.[41] Despite giving themselves an opportunity to decide whether the whole set of Vienna rules should apply the impression conveyed to, and taken up by, later courts was that to adopt and international law approach all that is required is to look at the 'preparatory work' of the treaty in question.[42]

Lord Diplock alone indicated that fuller application of the rules was mandated or, if he did not go that far, at least hinted at it. Lord Diplock said:

> international courts and tribunals do refer to travaux préparatoires as an aid to interpretation and this practice *as regards national courts* has now been confirmed by the Vienna Convention on the Law of Treaties (Cmnd. 4140), to which Her Majesty's Government is a party and which entered into force a few months ago. It applies only to treaties concluded after it came into force ...; but what it says in Articles 31 and 32 about interpretation of treaties, in my view, does no more than codify already-existing public international law.[43]

He then quoted the rules in Articles 31(1) and 32,[44] stating further on in his judgment:

> Accordingly, in exercising its interpretative function of ascertaining what it was that the delegates to an international conference agreed upon ... where the text is ambiguous or obscure, an English court should have regard to any material which the delegates themselves had thought would be available to clear up any possible ambiguities or obscurities. Indeed, in the case of Acts of Parliament giving effect to international conventions concluded after the coming into force

of [the Vienna Convention], I think an English court might well be under a constitutional obligation to do so.[45]

Leaving to one side the important point that 'rules' for interpretation may be no more than principles and that their application is not a mechanistic guarantee of reaching the 'correct' interpretation, since there are differences between the two sets of rules of interpretation the courts ought to decide which ones they are to apply in cases where treaties are considered. The differences in effect may not be great, though the role that is recognized in the international law rules for subsequent practice in the application of the treaty or the extent of recourse to supplementary means of interpretation (to give two examples) does demonstrate significant divergence between the sets of rules.[46]

Reverting to *Hiscox v Outhwaite*,[47] in the Court of Appeal Lord Donaldson MR had acknowledged that interpretation here warranted an approach that was not dictated by English case law: 'the convention and the Act giving effect to it do not fall to be considered in the light of the English law of arbitration'.[48] He nevertheless effectively sustained his conclusion by reference to *Brooke v Mitchell*,[49] as did the other judges in the Court of Appeal and House of Lords, notwithstanding that that case was remote from the issue, pre-dated the New York Convention by more than a century and could scarcely be said to be pertinent to its interpretation.

In marked contrast, at first instance Hirst J. adopted an approach based on interpretation of the treaty as it would be interpreted applying the international law rules. He quoted with approval an article by Dr F.A. Mann which included the statement: 'In so far as the Conventions ... are concerned, we know that Article 31 of the Vienna Convention governs their interpretation'.[50] Dr Mann's article from which these words were taken revealed a full application of the Vienna rules, achieving a conclusion which is probably more consistent with an interpretation of the kind that an international tribunal would give, rather than the narrow approach of the higher courts in England constrained by their focus on English law traditions of interpretation.

On the central question of where an arbitral award is 'made', Dr Mann showed that the proper interpretation of the treaty, placing due weight on the context as described in the Vienna rules, led one to the arbitral seat, or (summarizing) to the place that was the central point of the arbitral proceedings, as being the place where the award was made. This connotes the seat of the arbitration in a legal sense.[51] It was not simply a question of where the award happened to have been signed. Hirst J. accepted this and pointed out that the situation would have been different, and the meaning unambiguous, had the provision read 'signed' rather than 'made': 'One must' he said 'look at the arbitration as a whole, and not just the place of signature.'[52]

The question of whether there is an ambiguity in the words in the statute may be important in influencing the court's approach to the preparatory work of the treaty.[53] It is not entirely clear whether the courts now insist on such ambiguity or whether, if a treaty is involved, they might apply Article 32 of the Vienna Rules which envisages broader circumstances and further objectives justifying examining the preparatory work, including the search for confirmation of the meaning as well as establishing the meaning.[54]

In *Hiscox v Outhwaite* the ambiguity noted by Hirst J. was not stressed as a prerequisite in the higher courts for looking at the preparatory work. In any event, the judges in the Court of Appeal and House of Lords seem to have been blind to any meaning of 'made' other than that to which they were conditioned by their acquaintance with English law and practice. Probably to most English lawyers 'made' in connection with a legal instrument does have a clear meaning of 'executed', 'perfected' or (as in the present context) 'signed'. Yet the dictionary includes the definition of 'make' as 'to draw up (a legal document)'.[55] Thus the immediate ambiguity acknowledged by Hirst J. can be viewed as reinforced in that if that definition were applied, where the arbitrator 'drew up' his award is not necessarily the same place as where he signed it.

However, it is not in semantics that the questions and doubts arise in this area. The higher courts did look at the preparatory work but reverted to type in the manner of their examination of them and their preference for the English precedent. Yet uncharacteristically for preparatory work, in this case it was very clear what the delegates at the conference thought they were doing in the word they used (though the courts here did not recognize this).[56]

That is not to say that the intention of the delegates would displace a clear meaning or that their intention is what the Vienna rules identify as the holy grail in the quest for interpretation.[57] However, the precise solution in the instant case is not the real cause for concern here.[58] What is lacking is an indication of the basis on which the courts look at preparatory work and their object in doing so. In this case neither the Court of Appeal nor the House of Lords looked at the preparatory work in the manner in which someone applying Article 32 of the Vienna rules would assess it; nor did these courts accept the approach of someone familiar with international law, such as Dr Mann. For them, looking at the preparatory work seems to have been some forlorn exercise enjoined by the decision in *Fothergill v Monarch* as a nod in the direction of the public international law parentage of the provision in issue.

Thus *Hiscox v Outhwaite* provides a strong illustration of the unresolved uncertainty over interpretation which was engendered by *Fothergill v Monarch*. In the time between these two cases there have been a few others in which a passing reference has been made to the Vienna rules. In only one of these[59] has the analysis followed what might be retrospectively assessed as full application of the Vienna rules. This must, however, be viewed as most probably fortuitous since the reference to the rules only comes at a late stage in the judgment and in the context of justifying resort to consideration of an Explanatory Report accompanying a treaty.[60]

Conclusion

Problems remain over the interpretation of treaties in the United Kingdom for a number of reasons. The relationship between public international law and domestic law has never been adequately defined. The variety of methods of giving effect to treaties in legislation presents an unclear picture of whether the treaty or the legislation is the substantive instrument to be interpreted when the words in issue originate in the treaty; nor is it simply a question of the appearance of the legislation, that is whether the text of the treaty is reproduced or transformed.[61] An essential unresolved question is whether it is the treaty itself that is to be interpreted or the statutory reflection of it. Most telling of all is the failure of the courts to take a clear position on whether the ordinary rules of statutory interpretation or the rules of public international law in the Vienna Convention apply when considering words in, or taken from, a treaty.

Notes

1   No distinction is made or intended here or subsequently between the different jurisdictions within the United Kingdom. There is no obvious reason why interpretation of treaties should differ in the component parts of the realm. Rather, on the contrary, matters which are essentially the consequence of public international law should receive the same treatment. Perhaps because the separate jurisdictions should be uniform in their application of substantive provisions of international law and in their approach to the interpretation of treaties having effect in the United Kingdom, the judges in the House of Lords tend to refer to law in the United Kingdom and English law indiscriminately. When considering treaties, judges in Scottish courts appear to accommodate such usage: see the references by Lord Marnoch in *Abnett v British Airways* (Court of Session) [1996] SLT 529 to 'United Kingdom authority' and to *Fothergill v Monarch Airlines* (note 40 below), the latter being a case in which switches in terminology between 'United Kingdom' and 'England' abound. Similarly in *Abnett* in the Court of Session Inner House (First Division), Lord Mayfield also referred to *Fothergill v Monarch* without demur and concluded: 'It is no doubt desirable in matters of international application that uniform constructions should be achieved; ... it is at least satisfactory to reach a result which ... establishes a uniformity between Scotland and England on this issue' (at 547).

2   *Convention on the Law of Treaties signed at Vienna, 1969* (UK Treaty Series No. 58 (1980), Cmnd. 4140).

3   This use of the preparatory work of treaties was accepted well before the decision in *Pepper v Hart* [1993] AC 593 allowed the comparable, if more limited, examination of certain Parliamentary material.

4   See note 57 below.

5   See R. Higgins, *Problems and Process* (OUP, 1994), 206–208.

6   See for example *Triquet v Bath* (1764) 3 Burr. 1478: 'Lord Talbot declared a clear opinion – "That the law of nations in its full extent was part of the law of England, ... that the law of nations was to be collected from the practice of different nations and the authority of writers".' (per Lord Mansfield, 97 ER 936 at 938.)

7   See A. Coates, *Myself a Mandarin* (OUP, 1968), pp. 123–146.

8   [1977] QB 529 at 554.

9   Loc. cit. at pp. 553–4.

10 In addressing terminology, it may also be appropriate to note that 'treaty' is a term used here to describe international agreements between states (and less frequently international organizations) and governed by public international law. Many other terms are used to describe treaties, including convention, agreement, protocol, act, covenant etc.

11 See F.A.R. Bennion, *Statutory Interpretation: a Code* (Butterworths, 2nd edn., 1992) at p. 459: 'an Act may embody, whether or not in the same words, provisions having the effect of the treaty (in this Code referred to as direct enactment of the treaty)'.

12 This is commonly the case with treaties on extradition and double taxation.

13 Bennion, op. cit., at pp. 460–461. Bennion seems to suggest that what he describes as direct enactment is preferable to using the actual text of the treaty, the former leading to 'precision drafting' while the latter uses 'disorganised composition' and 'sloppy' drafting. Unfortunately, in the example he gives of the former, the Arbitration Act 1975, the words used in the legislation as interpreted by the House of Lords in *Hiscox v Outhwaite* [1992] 1 AC 562 (considered below), were no advance on those in the treaty.

14 See *J.H. Rayner (Mincing Lane) v Dept of Trade* [1990] 2 AC 418 at 500, citing *Fothergill v. Monarch* [1981] 2 AC 548.

15 See the comments in the text above on the meaning ascribed to 'direct' and 'indirect' enactment. In *Fothergill v Monarch Airways* (cited above), on which Lord Oliver was basing his remark, the relevant statute (the Carriage by Air Act 1961) set out the text of the Convention in a Schedule (albeit, when amended, with certain statutory accretions).

16 The extent of this presumption is explained in *R v Secretary of State Ex parte Brind* [1991] 1 AC 699. The presumption could not be used to ensure that exercise of a discretion conformed to the European Convention for Protection of Human Rights and Fundamental Freedoms which has not been incorporated into domestic law. Lord Bridge said: 'the presumption ... is a mere canon of construction which involves no importation of international law into the domestic field' (loc. cit. at p. 748). Particular considerations bearing on the interpretation of this European Convention and the treaties on the European Communities and European Union are not taken up here. These treaties set up their own interpretative mechanisms which, as regards their relationship to the internal order of the United Kingdom and their treatment in the English courts, rather sets them apart from other treaties.

17 [1983] 2 AC 548.

18 Ibid. at 564–565.

19 See for example section 2 of the Carriage by Air and Road Act 1979 which gave a

legislative interpretation of the same provisions which had been in issue in *Fothergill v Monarch* loc. cit.

20 See sections 8 and 9 of the International Transport Conventions Act 1983 which provide for amended versions of transport conventions to be given effect by Order in Council. See also the Asylum and Immigration Appeals Act 1993, considered in the text below. In a much more extensive way, legislation giving effect to the treaties on the European Communities has provided for a continuing process of implementation. This far-reaching body of law has led to strange perceptions of contrast with other legislation implementing treaties. In *Quazi v Quazi* [1980] AC 744 at p. 775, referring to the Hague Convention on Recognition of Divorces and Legal Separations, Wood J. said: 'This Convention although not a treaty nor indeed a provision of law within the European Economic Community nevertheless is something which I am satisfied I can examine in order to seek the true meaning of the provisions of the Act itself.'

21 Section 1 of the 1993 Act states: '"The Convention" means the Convention relating to the Status of Refugees done at Geneva on 28th July 1951 and the Protocol to that Convention.' For the effect of the 1993 Act, see *R v Secretary of State for the Home Department, ex p. Mehari and others* [1994] QB 474, Laws J. at 489:

> As regards domestic law, before the Act was passed, the Secretary of State had undertaken by the then current immigration rules in effect to abide by the Convention. Section 2 of the statute merely requires that he should do the same thing in the future. Under the pre-existing regime the government had created at any rate a legitimate expectation that the Secretary of State would not remove an asylum seeker from the United Kingdom where to do so would, or perhaps reasonably might, expose him to persecution: whatever the reach of the obligation not thus to remove a claimant, it is not lengthened by section 2 of the 1993 Act.

22 See note 21 above. See also *Thavathevathasan v Secretary of State for the Home Department* [1994] Immig. AR 249; *Secretary of State for the Home Department v Khalif Mohamed Abdi* [1994] Immig. AR 402; and *R v Secretary of State for the Home Department, ex p. Khan and others* [1995] 2 All ER 540.

23 In *Salomon v Commissioners of Customs & Excise* [1967] 2 QB 116 the Court of Appeal accepted that even where an Act makes no mention of a treaty, cogent extrinsic evidence to connect the treaty with the Act would permit the Court to look at the treaty to elucidate the Act.

24 See R Higgins in F.G. Jacobs and S. Roberts (eds), *The Effect of Treaties in Domestic Law* (Sweet & Maxwell, 1987), at p. 133.

25 *Salomon* per Diplock L.J., loc. cit. at p. 143.

26 Report of the Law Commission on *The Interpretation of Statutes* (Law. Com. Report No. 21), 1969, p. 10, para. 14.

27 See *Hiscox v Outhwaite* [1992] 1 AC 562 and text to note 52 below.

28 [1978] AC 547.

29 [1985] 1 AC 58.

30 The Convention on the Taking of Evidence Abroad in Civil or Commercial Matters, The Hague, 1970.

31 Article 23 of the Convention allowed certain evidence to be excluded from compliance with letters of request. Article 12(b) allowed the court to have regard to possible prejudice to the sovereignty of the United Kingdom. See per Lord Wilberforce, loc. cit. at pp. 608 and 616.

32 Loc. cit.

33 See *Panam v Dept of Trade* [1976] 1 Lloyd's Rep. 257.

34   See further R. K. Gardiner, 'Air Law's Fog: The Application of International and English Law', (1990) 43 CLP 159.
35   [1990] 2 AC 418.
36   The International Tin Council (Immunities and Privileges) Order, 1972 SI No. 120, Article 2.
37   Further investigation of these issues and additional cases can be found in R. K. Gardiner, 'Treaty Interpretation in the English Courts since *Fothergill v Monarch Airlines (1980)*', (1995) 44 ICLQ 620.
38   [1992] 1 AC 562.
39   Section 7.
40   [1981] AC 251.
41   See Article 26 of the amended Convention on Unification of Certain Rules relating to Carriage by Air, Warsaw, 1929 ('the Warsaw Convention') as set out in the First Schedule to the Carriage by Air Act 1961.
42   'Preparatory work' is the term used in Article 32 of the Vienna Convention though the English judiciary appears to prefer the French term *travaux préparatoires*. The term is not defined in the Convention. Lord McNair in *The Law of Treaties* (OUP, 1961), at p. 411, describes the 'preparatory work' as 'an omnibus expression which is used rather loosely to indicate all the documents, such as memoranda, minutes of conferences, and drafts of the treaty under negotiation'. Referring to the conference at which the Warsaw Convention was adopted, Lord Scarman said:

> Working papers of delegates to the conference, or memoranda submitted by the delegates for consideration by the conference, though relevant, will seldom be helpful; but an agreed conference minute of the understanding on the basis of which the draft of an article of the convention was accepted may well be of great value.' (*Fothergill v Monarch*, loc. cit. at 294).

43   Loc. cit. at 282 with emphasis added.
44   The Vienna rules (UK Treaty Series No. 58 (1980), Cmnd. 4140) state:

Article 31
General rule of interpretation

1)   A treaty shall be interpreted in good faith in accordance with the ordinary meaning to be given to the terms of the treaty in their context and in the light of its object and purpose.

2)   The context for the purpose of the interpretation of a treaty shall comprise, in addition to the text, including its preamble and annexes:
     a)   any agreement relating to the treaty which was made between all the parties in connexion with the conclusion of the treaty;
     b)   any instrument which was made by one or more of the parties in connexion with the conclusion of the treaty and accepted by the other parties as an instrument related to the treaty.

3)   There shall be taken into account, together with the context:
     a)   any subsequent agreement between the parties regarding the interpretation of the treaty or the application of its provisions;
     b)   any subsequent practice in the application of the treaty which establishes the agreement of the parties regarding its interpretation;

    c)   any relevant rules of international law applicable in the relations between the parties.

4)   A special meaning shall be given to a term if it is established that the parties so intended.

Article 32
Supplementary means of interpretation

Recourse may be had to supplementary means of interpretation, including the preparatory work of the treaty and the circumstances of its conclusion, in order to confirm the meaning resulting from the application of Article 31, or to determine the meaning when the interpretation according to Article 31:
a)   leaves the meaning ambiguous or obscure; or
b)   leads to a result which is manifestly absurd or unreasonable.

(Article 33, applicable where a treaty is in more than one language, is not reproduced here.)

45   *Id.* at 283.
46   The Law Commission in its Report on interpretation of statutes (see note 26 above) clearly did see a divergence. The Commission noted its hope that the clarifications and modifications which it recommended 'may help narrow any gap between the general interpretative approach of our courts and that required by international law in relation to the interpretation of treaties' (loc. cit., p. 45, para. 76). It also recommended, however, that the matter should be further considered after the completion of the work of the diplomatic conference on the law of treaties (which led to the Vienna Convention, then only in draft).
47   Loc. cit. note 38 above.
48   [1992] 1 Lloyd's Rep. 1 at 13.
49   (1840) 6 M & W 473.
50   The quotation is in [1991] 2 Lloyd's Rep. 1, 7–8. For F.A. Mann's comment on the decision of the House of Lords see 108 (1992) LQR 6. See also F.P. Davidson, 'Where is an Arbitral Award Made? – *Hiscox v Outhwaite*', 41 (1992) ICLQ 637 and C. Reymond, 'Where is an Arbitral Award Made?', 108 (1992) LQR 1.
51   See Reymond, loc. cit. at p. 638.
52   Loc. cit. at p. 8.
53   See *Salomon v Commissioners of Customs & Excise*, note 23 above.
54   See text of Article 32 in note 44 above.
55   Shorter Oxford English Dictionary.
56   The United Kingdom's delegate supported the initial draft put to the conference ('arbitral award made in the territory of a state') as providing 'an objective and easily applicable criterion'. The American delegate supported this as in the USA 'it was *the place of arbitration* which determined whether an award was a foreign award' (emphasis added). The United Kingdom's delegate (who had supported a geographical test) did not demur from the US delegate's interpretation of this draft rule E/CONF.26/SR.5 in G. Gaja, *International Commercial Arbitration* (Oceana, 1978), Vol. III at III.C.29–30 and Supplements). This was also the understanding of Working Party No.1 (see E/CONF.26/ L.42 and III.B.4.2) to which the matter was referred. The working party found that the views of governments fell into two categories:

a)   those favouring 'the principle of the place of arbitration'; and
b)   those favouring the principle of nationality of the arbitral award.

In reconciling these views the working party recommended wording in all material particulars the same as that ultimately in the convention. It seems clear that 'awards made in the territory of a state' reflected (a) above (place of arbitration), while a second sentence was added to Article 1 to reflect (b). The UK delegate was a member of the working party and did not record any dissent from the working party's report.

57   In *Swiss Bank Corp v Brink's-MAT* [1986] QB 853 at 857. Bingham J. decided he should approach the convention in question 'in an objective spirit in order to try to discover what its true intent is'. The Vienna Convention rules do not include a reference to intent of the parties in the general rule. The Vienna Conference, in considering the draft Vienna rules, noted with approval that 'the [International Law] Commission … came down firmly in favour of the view that "the starting point of interpretation is the elucidation of the meaning of the text, not an investigation *ab initio* into the intentions of the parties".' However, Bingham J.'s approach looks for the intent of the treaty, not of the parties. Though this does not follow exactly the Vienna Convention, it may be close to it. Nevertheless, if the Vienna rules apply, it would be more appropriate to use the actual wording of the relevant rule rather than constructing another rule which may happen to be somewhat like it.

58   Commentators have reacted strongly to the substance of the decision: for example 'nothing short of being a truly startling conclusion' (Rhydian Thomas, 'Reflections on Recent Judicial Development of the Concept of a Convention Award', (1992) 11 CJQ 352 at p. 358); 'While the view that an award is made at the seat of arbitration attributes a somewhat strained meaning to the word "made", the interpretation favoured by the House of Lords has profound implications and may lead to bizarre results' (J. Hill, *The Law Relating to International Commercial Disputes* (Lloyd's of London Press, 1994), at p. 531.)

59   *Read v Secretary of State for the Home Department* [1988] 3 All ER 993.

60   Lord Bridge gave the sole judgment with which the other judges concurred. Of the Explanatory Report he said 'it is available as an aid to construction as part of the "travaux préparatoires" and under Article 31 of the Vienna Convention on the Law of Treaties' (loc. cit. at 999).

61   Dr Mann has commented on the method of legislation by which the language of the treaty is transformed into 'statutory' language:

But whether or not the method is atypical it is entirely different from the situation … in which Parliament 'is, broadly speaking, merely machinery rather than the source of law' or, in other words, 'is not the real law-giver, but merely the law-transformer', the treaty itself being the (indirect) source of law. (F.A. Mann, *Further Studies in International Law* (OUP, 1990), p. 271.)

8 Interpretation and Commitment in Legal Reasoning

Stephen Guest*

The idea of commitment runs through all human activities and my argument will be, in the particular, that interpretation in law and the arts are identical in being a practice in which judgments are made about commitments with which the interpreter engages and shares. Interpretation is thus (to use a metaphor which will only later be apparent as that) to be seen as a joint venture between an author (who may be a group) and an interpreter. I shall further argue that although the ideas of intention and meaning have a significant role in the identification of the thing-to-be-interpreted, it has a much less significant role, if any role, in the interpretation itself. That both of these propositions is true is strikingly apparent in law from a consideration of the widely used idea of legislative intention in the interpretation of statutes.

Two things follow, I think, from seeing interpretation as a form of commitment. First, no great significance should be attached to drawing a distinction between what might be called the 'matrix' of the law (the legislators, the production of the written law, the decisions, the legislative history and so forth) and those who make the interpretations (the academic, the judge, the law student) since all must engage to some extent with the commitments of all. Likewise with the arts, there is no great significance in the distinction between the author(s) and the critic and the performer, since they, too, are committed in much the same way. Second, understanding interpretation in this way should encourage realization of the immense imaginative possibilities (including the critical) of *departing* from (or *re-introducing*) generally accepted interpretive views, thus allowing for unorthodox and novel interpretations.

Intention and Meaning

A strong sense we have of interpretation is one which connects it to the idea of meaning. This sense relies upon an idea of things-having-meaning and of our making some sort of extension or restriction to that meaning. It is therefore reasonable to suppose that it is wrong to equate interpretation with *translation*, since a translator, as opposed to an interpreter, aims to reproduce as far as possible in identical form the meanings as understood in one language into another. Further, since interpretation must be interpretation *of* something, the truth of an interpretation is clearly connected with the truth of the thing interpreted. That this is so is apparent from what we do when we extend or restrict ordinary understandings. Say we interpret 'Vehicles are prohibited in the park' not to include a prohibition on skateboards, it would be nonsense to suppose that we no longer accept that, after our interpretation, it is not true that all vehicles are prohibited in the park just because skateboards are permitted. Our interpretation of the meaning of 'Vehicles are prohibited in the park' requires our continued acceptance of the truth of the proposition that all vehicles are prohibited.[1] In this way interpretation is more constrained, or tied back, than either improvisation or free invention and so on. In sum, although interpretation is not translation it would be quite wrong to equate it with anything approaching licence.

There is clearly, too, a close relationship between the idea of meaning and that of what an author intended by something. Although I shall largely be talking about statutory (and judicial) language I do not believe my remarks only apply to those human artefacts expressed in words. Nevertheless, a central case of interpretation is the speaker's intention sense and I am inclined to assimilate many cases of interpretation to this central case. Roughly, Grice's well-known definition works sufficiently here: 'to say that a speaker S meant something by X is to say that S intended by the utterance of X to produce some effect in a hearer H by means of the recognition of this intention'. Basically, this is to say that meaning depends on your recognition of the speaker's intention.[2]

Scientific Interpretation

It is – possibly – problematic to assimilate intention to the scientific interpretation of data, but I do not think that anything I say need account for this sort of interpretation. Interpretation of events in the world which had not been created by an author (I exclude God) does not clearly, at any rate, seem assimilable to any form of intentional activity. We can try: it may be that scientists regard such interpretation in the sense in which, acting within the scientist's (the scientific *author*) created hypotheses (for example Newton's law of physics), they search for a meaning there to explain outside phenomena. That seems to me to be a reasonable way forward since it seems right that the data to be interpreted is data as-determined-by-an-intentionally-created theory. (In other words, 'data' does not exist 'out there'.) On the other hand, there is a forced artificiality about the idea since scientific theories in the end purport to be about the world and not other theories. But I do not intend to pursue here the precise nature of scientific analysis.

Meaning as Importance or Significance

We should also put to one side, for present purposes, a sense of 'meaning' which accounts for the importance something has in a person's life. You go to a lawyer (as happened to me) and ask whether he is a specialist in the Landlord and Tenant Act 1987. In particular, you are interested in what certain sections of that statute mean in relation to your own special circumstances and you check with the solicitor that he is acquainted with this statute and these provisions. In my case, the lawyer said that the statute 'meant' a lot to him. What he actually meant was that the particular statute represented an important event in his life since, as an MP, he had been responsible for piloting it, as a bill, through its final legislative stages. The Landlord and Tenant Act 1987 meant something to him in the sense that it represented an important project in his life. And there is the obvious sense of 'mean' when you say that your wife or husband *means* a lot to you, or when you say that life is 'full of *meaning*'.

The Thing Interpreted

The speaker's intending by something is a central sense of meaning and usefully draws attention to an artefact – something created by the speaker – the 'thing to be interpreted'. This sense rules out driftwood, or beautiful stones, or miraculous sunsets, or people's bodies as art. There is an important sense in which what marks out the legal enactment or the work of art is that it is intentionally created as the enactment or the work of art.[3] This sense rules out just any artefact whatsoever amounting to art. In this sense, the creator controls to at least some significant extent the criteria of assessment of what he produces although the creation can in both law and art take on a life of its own which may diverge from what the creator intended. The sense of control is important, however, since it accounts for the strong pull we have towards the idea that the creator (the author/the artist/the composer/the legislator/the judge) has some authority over his creation. It is not just that it would be odd if it were not at all important to pay attention to the way Shostakovich conducted one of his symphonies; it would be bizarre if a conductor told his orchestra to ignore the notes that Shostakovich had actually written!

To see intention as relating to the creation of something special in this area draws our attention to the rules and practices which define the way of expressing meaning, for example, statutory meaning. I think it helps to make clear why we would tend to disregard 'off the record' remarks by an MP to a television interviewer or the notebook jottings of poets as part of the work. More plausible cases, however, are: taking into account statements of public record such as Law Commission Reports, or special committees (see *R v Bull*, in which 'prostitute' was interpreted not to refer to male prostitute, after confirmation by reference to the Wolfenden Committee which drafted the relevant provision[4]) or *Hansard* proceedings (*Pepper v Hansard* according to which courts can now look at *Hansard* when there is ambiguity, obscurity or absurdity[5]), or various corrected drafts of plays, or newly discovered scores of parts of symphonies.[6] Another way of getting at the idea that there can be something there which has its own identity independent of those intentions, thoughts, purposes and so on is by drawing an analogy with promise-keeping. You can fail to promise by, say, the telephone going dead unbeknownst to you as you make the promise. You have not, in these cases, successfully produced the thing with a life of its own. But once the promise is successfully made, it stands on its own: you cannot later negate your promise by saying that when you promised you did not mean it. The standard complaint to be made to someone who has broken a promise is simply 'You promised'.

The speaker's intention idea is a popular idea of meaning in the understanding of statutes and since one of the major tasks of lawyers is the interpretation of statutes, I shall look at this question. But again, qualification is required. Note that statutory interpretation is different from interpreting the common law where characteristically there is no canonical form of words or even a clearly definable event as speaking.[7] A useful way of understanding the difference between the two is to consider the child who understands that he is not to take the dog to bed with him by either paying attention to Dad's words 'Fido is not to go to bed with you' (Dad's statute) or to Dad's, Mum's and sister's previous behaviour when he has taken the dog to bed: 'You gave Cordelia £5 and she was naughty and I didn't get smacked last time I took Fido to bed' (an argument within the 'common law' of the Robinson family). It was because of this relatively unclear and uncertain way of directing behaviour that Bentham thought that legislation was much superior to the common law, incidentally.

Parliamentary Intention

Intention not only fails to explain or justify many interpretative decisions in its name, but it leads decision-makers to regard the law as existing independent of their individual judgments about what a legislative body is entitled to do. The idea, at best a metaphor, suggests both the existence of a physical *mind* and what is going on 'in' that mind – a psychological state. An examination of these two entities, too, is a matter for historical research, and that alone. Let us try it: finding an historic intention entails an enormously difficult task in law, as well as art, simply because the large proportion of authors are dead. Extending the point to art, if all artistic interpretations were the discovery of artists' intentions then what a dreary business artistic and literary criticism becomes. Nevertheless, exploration of artistic intentions is one canon of artistic interpretation and, regrettably, in my view, leads to the kind of scholarship which is productive of such historical facts as that Shakespeare was in fact another person, or it was Salieri, not Mozart, who wrote the operas. But there are more obvious problems with the idea and these need to be considered in turn.

Group Problems

Parliamentary intention seems different from artistic intention in that the intentions of a large number of people are involved, although there are artistic endeavours which involve groups, notably writing serial plays. (I realize that some people think that such artistic endeavours are in some way inferior for that reason.) Nevertheless, in some sense, an orchestra plays with a certain group intention in mind, likewise with dance groups and the players in plays. It is possible to dismiss the whole idea of Parliamentary intention just on the ground that group intentions are impossible because two or more people cannot share the same mental state; but it may be too quick. People can share the same intention at least in the sense that they have very similar intentions at the same time.

More problematic cases are the usual kind, however, where separate members of the legislature have different intentions. There are a number of possible combinations. One possibility is that the intention of Parliament is that shared by those who voted for the successful bill. But it is important to remember that it is the bill itself that shows the intention. Since this is so, those members in the opposition who voted against the bill *just because* they understood the bill to have the majority's meaning could also be counted amongst those who have the requisite Parliamentary intention. If it is *not* the case that not all those who voted for the bill read it the same way, therefore, the possibility arises that the meaning of the bill as judged by a majority in

Parliament will arise from a cross-party intention. When interpreting the statute, what should we choose? It will depend on a judgment which, independently of what these intentions are, sorts these intentions out in a way that makes no reference to intention at all.

Despite these arguments, the difficulties should not be overstated to conclude that any idea of Parliamentary intention is a nonsense; there are clearly uncontentious statutes with clear meanings which are clearly assented to by both sides of the House and there is not too much difficulty, at least at a common-sense level, in talking of a shared intention. If we ignore philosophy for a bit, we will find it useful, at least for present purposes, to consider the possibility of shared intentions lying at the basis of statutory interpretation.

However, even if we concede that there are group intentions of this type, we are faced with a problem of the continuity of Parliament. Parliament enacted the Metropolitan Police Act 1837, which forbids the repair of carriages (when there has been a complaint) within the Metropolitan Police District, long before Parliament (viewed as the group-mind-existing-then) could possibly have foreseen that cars would be invented. When we examine the idea of parliamentary intention now as to whether a criminal offence has been committed by someone repairing a car, it is not clear how 'intention' helps us in any significant way. Parliament exists now as it did then. Assuming the group-mind view of Parliament, let us distinguish two parliaments: the one that existed then in 1837 and the one that exists now in 1995. Which intention counts? The question makes us wonder whether the distinction makes sense. If we take the view that Parliament consists, not of its members, but of the institution defined in terms of rules, practices and conventions which define, amongst various duties, powers and capacities, certain offices which members from time to time fill, then 'Parliament' means now what it meant then.[8] We cannot draw the distinction and instead are required to make a judgment about whether, given that Parliament produced, in 1837, a statutory provision relating to 'carriages', that is a reason, in the absence of any competing reason (such as many modern statutes specifically exempting cars from blanket provisions relating to vehicles), for declaring that it is an offence to repair a car.

This way of putting things removes any reference to the idea of intention. In other words, this suggests that we can do without it. Of course, there are problems that remain but with the idea of intention removed we gain clarity in what is being asked of an interpreter. Instead of asking 'What intention did Parliament have in 1837?' (which tends to hide a process of reasoning), we consider full frontally the question: 'What present force is there in the argument "that Parliament produced ... in 1837"?' As I have suggested, the answer lies in the idea of "what is Parliament committed to' although I have yet to flesh this idea out. But since the idea of intention is so widely used, it is useful to press on with the difficulties in the idea of Parliamentary intention. Let us assume that continuing group continuity problems are not real problems, at least for the time being. For there are more difficulties that have to be faced.

Whose Intention?

The pressure group's intention in bringing the problem to the MP's notice? After all, the pressure group characteristically consists of the group of people most acquainted with the nature of the problem which the statute seeks to solve. Or is it the intention of the committee of civil servants who produced the draft and accompanying explanation for the legislative draftsman? Or, as is sometimes suggested, the intention of the legislative draftsman himself? What about the legislator who voted with a particular understanding of how the bill was intended to be understood?

The question arises: by what means do we choose the correct person? Some accounts try to develop the ideas of agency and trust here, so that the *legislative draftsman's* intention is the primary target for understanding. This draftsman is seen as an agent for his Parliamentary principal who, in turn, acts in trust to his constituents and acts both as part agent for the lobbyists and part agent for the civil servants. But it is clear – is it not – that these are contortions. They cannot work to ground the appropriate intention for the very simple reason that the criteria specifying *whose* intention is to count are left unspecified. These are not intention-based criteria for saying why the conceptions of trust and agency are required, or appropriate here, as a supplementary account. Obviously, we cannot find the appropriate intention by referring to another statute and the parliamentary intention in that as to whose intention counts. Indeed, interpretation statutes are notoriously unhelpful. If there were a statute specifying whose intention was to count that statute itself would be open to the same question. In a nutshell: saying so does not make it so. (Crudely: if Parliament declared that shellfish had intentions, it would not mean that shellfish now had intentions; merely that Parliament had declared that shellfish had intentions.) Of course, all this is not to say there are no clear rules establishing how statutes are to be produced. There obviously are. It is just that these rules could not establish that the intention conception of statutory meaning is true, although it is a surprisingly common view that such statutes can.

What, then, are the criteria of relevance in determining what obligations and so on, statutory provisions establish? First, we could make a judgment about the relative worth of the lobbyist's intentions, or the civil servants' intentions and the legislator's intention and resolve it by saying that the legislator's intention is more important since the legislator has a duty to make an independent judgment of worth of the lobbyist's wants in the light of his position as an elected representative. But it is important to see that this is a judgment of political morality and not a judgment of historical enquiry. Take *R v Registrar-General, ex parte Smith*.[9] S.51 of the Adoption Act 1976 states 'The Registrar-General shall on application by an adopted person supply to that person a certified copy of the record of his birth'. The applicant was refused such information on the ground that there was evidence that he intended to find out who his natural mother was so that he could murder her. He naturally argued that he had an 'absolute right' to the information but the Court of Appeal said that Parliament could not have intended that the right be absolute where the information might lead to the commission of a serious crime. Lobbyists, if there were any, may have intended that absolute rights be granted and the legislator may have modified that by intending that s.51 be read non-absolutely where there was a genuine risk of serious crime. But in interpreting these words, how would we choose? Different judgments, *not* about what-Parliament-intended-in-a-historical-sense, are required. For example, placing weight on a principle of certainty in legislation produces a different judgment from that where some other principle had greater weight, say, the protection of innocent people.

Secondly, we need to consider the reasons for regarding the bill as produced by the legislator and not as produced in the initiating stages as primary. One judgment we might reasonably make is simply the practical concern that statute production requires an artificial narrowing of issues so as to save time and expense and encourage conciseness and clarity. Another judgment it would be reasonable to make is on a clear democratic principle of accountability focusing on the written record the responsibility for which lies on the elected representatives. (It would be judgment of this kind, incidentally, that would turn us naturally to suppose that it is the majority who voted for the successful bill whose intention counts.) It seems clear from these arguments the criteria of whose intention counts requires more than reference to mental events and instead requires some sort of judgment over and above such events. Crudely, the idea we should reject is that there is no intention 'out there' which is ready-labelled 'I am the requisite intention'.[10]

What Precise Mental State?

This problem is the most acute, even in the shared intention case, since criteria have to be specified as to what intention precisely is being shared. A legislator might have several intentions in relation to the successful bill, as well as accompanying related mental states. He might have voted for the bill without having understood its provisions, his intention in doing so only being to please the whips; or his intention might have been to support the bill solely because his wife had business interests that would be furthered; or, more complicatedly, he may have had the various intentions of pleasing the whips, furthering the business interests of his wife (who is a director of a water authority) and ensuring that the environment would be improved.

Again which is the relevant intention? These differing intentions aside, there are further problems arising from the fact that mental states other than intention may be just as appropriate in working out what the statute means. The legislator may *foresee* that the statute will be read one way but *hope* that it will be read another way. Further, his expectations and hopes may only be understood in the light of his *motives* for supporting what he knew to be ambiguous phrases. And when we delve into the murky mud of motives we may find that we are looking to those of the subconscious Marx/ Freudian bent, as where the legislator *false*-consciously votes for a statute since it serves a class interest, or *sub*-consciously votes in a particular way on a restrictive law on homosexual activity because it satisfies some re-pressed sexual urge. To repeat the argument, sorting out all these mental states requires something of entirely different order from an historical enquiry.

Imaginary Intention and the Problem of Gaps

In many cases there will be no requisite candidate for intention. Intention involves the idea of knowing and legislators, not being all-knowing, just do not foresee the sorts of situations which may arise nor how they should be dealt with. As Hart puts it in *The Concept of Law* it is a feature of the human predicament that we suffer from a 'relative ignorance of fact' and a 'relative indeterminacy of aim'.[11] It is because of this that there are many situations (where intentionally produced statements are relevant) over which interpret-ation questions hover. We might then ask what the legislator would have intended had he been asked. This clearly will not produce answers in every case, but it is not difficult to imagine the possibility. Austin thought for example that the judge's authority only extended to what the legislator had tacitly commanded. In the sort of gap being considered, the judge had to put himself in the position of the legislator and make a judgment about what the legislator would have commanded had he been in the court. (And so Aus-tin's famous declaration that the legal system would not last for half an hour if judges could not legislate has to be interpreted restrictively. The judges could not do what Parliament would not have wanted them to do).

But how do you ask the question? Take the Adoption Act case again. Consider the question: 'How would you have voted had you known what the circumstances of *Smith*'s case?' Ignoring the differing intentions problem where 'I'd have satisfied the whips' could be an answer, the question is still too general. If the legislator said that he would still have voted for the bill had he known, the answer is too wide, since the answer 'yes' leaves us with an ambiguity as to how *Smith*'s case should be decided. Instead, we have to put an imaginary amendment to the bill and ask the legislator, had he known about *Smith*, would he have voted for this amendment? But even this refinement is insufficient because we have to be careful about the wording. On the other hand, it might be unclear that the legislator would have voted an amendment phrased just in the specific terms of the problem as in: 'absolute with an exception for potential murderers of persons named on the birth certificate'. He might only have been prepared to consider a more general amendment along the lines of dealing with *Smith*'s case 'in exceptional circumstances' or 'in circumstances which leads to an injustice'. Again, which intention the legislator has is dependent upon the independent judgment being made about what type of question is put to him.

Commitment

From these considerations, I propose to abandon reference to the idea of intention and turn to the idea of commitment.

Commitment and Purpose

'Purpose' does not seem to be the right idea in this context although it is clearly relevant. The main problem with it is that there can be conflicting purposes which a statute attempts to reconcile in the normative form of describing how things should be. We can talk of 'the' purpose of the Criminal Evidence Act 1898 as that of reconciling two conflicting purposes, namely, to protect the defendant from prejudice and to remove the defendant's right not to incriminate himself. But similar sorts of problems arise here as with the idea of intention. 'What was Parliament's purpose?' and 'What was Parliament's intention?' are questions that are not as clear as the alternative argued for here: 'What is our legal system (of which I am a part) committed to, given (amongst many other things) that it says in s.1(e) and s.1(f) and so on?' Of course, it is not that the ideas of intention and purpose are *irrelevant*. That a person has a particular intention, or is acting on purpose, is good evidence of that person's commitments, and there can be no great harm in supposing that Parliamentary intention could be understood to *mean* Parliamentary commitment. But 'intention' carries with it all sorts of mental and historical baggage which needs to be discarded should this sort of adjustment to the concept of intention be adopted.

Statutory interpretation as capturing the historical intentions of legislators just does not make great sense. Why, though, does it fundamentally not work? It is that intentional concepts in ordinary lawyerlike use are too close to the idea of historic mental states – actual states of awareness which can be historically described and located – and too far away from the appropriate description of the legislator's commitment to the process by which legislation is produced. Further, understanding what a legislator is committed to unites two, as it were, 'subjective' judgments, that of the interpreter *and* that of the legislator. I think that it is essential to statutory interpretation for the interpreter to become like the legislator; this is the appeal of the idea of 'deciding in the legislator's shoes' – Austin's idea of the court deciding in accordance with the sovereign's tacit command.

But there is a stronger idea being pursued here, an idea not captured by 'intention' since intentions, consisting of essentially mental states, are not transferable or substitutable. Consider the following example, which draws from Quine's discussion of opaque contexts.[12] 'Q intends to shoot the first person to come through the gap; unbeknownst to him, the first person who will come through the gap is his wife; therefore Q intends to kill his wife.' This is a (logically) invalid argument. On the other hand, 'Q is committed to shooting the first person who comes through the gap; unbeknownst to him, the first person who will come through the gap is his wife; therefore he is committed to killing his wife' is a valid argument. Here the commitment *transfers* and we are able to say to the gunman that he was committed to shooting his wife despite his having no intentions in relation to the matter.

Of course, we have to be very careful here. It is easy to slip into the idea (because of the compelling nature of the example) to saying that 'commitment' is like 'intention' here because a person's having an intention in relation to X marks out that person's commitment to a particular action, meaning that, although a person might be surprised by the consequences of their action, that was in fact what followed from what they intended. But this cannot be right. Q might not have acted had he known what consequences his action was leading him to; he would say, as an excuse, 'I didn't intend that!' And blame, too, is not the issue here. We understand Q to have been committed to a course of action in which certain consequences follow and we can read his contribution to the consequences without reference to his mental state. Commitment is transferable, substitutable and transparent; intention and its cognates are opaque.

There are simpler, less technical, ways of expressing this point. So many examples are supplied by the law. Take, for example, the Metropolitan Police Act 1837 according to which 'carriages' must not be repaired within the Metropolitan Police District. The Act clearly (as far as we can say these things) applies to cars, even though no one in England then had any idea then that cars would be invented, and so no one could have had the (historic-) intention that the provision apply to cars.

In other words, we can make judgments about what a person is committed to and, further, we can, very importantly, *correct* what a person claims he is committed to. If Q denied he was committed to shooting his wife and claimed he was committed to shooting the first person who comes through the gap, one thing amongst others we can say is that he is mistaken in what he declares he is committed to. This should put us on guard against assuming that *bona fide* declarations as to what they intend or what they are committed to by politicians are conclusive as to what they are in fact committed to. This idea, of correcting what Parliament has done, as it does not cohere with the meaning of Parliament in its broadest sense, is just the sort of thing that can occur in art. There is no reason why an author should not be genuinely informed of how his work can be interpreted even if he had not actually that intention in mind when he wrote it.

The ruling idea here is, as I have suggested, that of commitment.[13] This requires us to make judgments about what a legislator is committed to independently of an historical enquiry into the mental state of that legislator. These judgments should be made on the basis of not only other acts in which the legislator is involved but on the basis of – in some important sense – engaging with the legislator's commitments. This is why we talk of the 'spirit' of legislation. We have to understand him (and, of course, for law this means to understand him in his official sense) to understand his judgments and what he is committed to.[14] (For present purposes, I am not interested in the discussion as to whether 'committed to' can be taken in a 'detached' or 'committed' way. We understand what *we*, ourselves, are committed to; we further easily understand what another person is committed to, *without ourselves being committed*. What I say does not depend on collapsing this distinction.)

The Power in the Idea of Commitment

In an unpleasant scene in the film *Schindler's List* the camp commander places his hand on the head of a Jewish girl (in a way, the only time he really *looks* at her) he is about to assault and says to her, wonderingly, 'You don't look like a rat'. But it lasts only momentarily and he treats her abominably – although not in fact as though she were a rat. Is it possible for us, from outside as it were, to correct his judgment and say that, despite what he appears to think, how he acts, what he intends to do, he is not really *committed* to the view that she is as expendable as a rat?

One way we could achieve the judgment would be by determining his consistency, or how rational he is in other ways. I do not suppose it would ever be convincing to say that, despite the way he talks, thinks and acts he does not really *mean* his acts. But we could tackle the problem another way. We could say that, although he means to do the terrible things he does, and genuinely *believes* that Jews are as much a part of the moral world as rats, the other commitments he has shown in his life, of self-discipline, of love of companionship, of devotion to music and so on, the two sides to him are inconsistent. Could we go so far as to say that he is not really committed to the view that she really is not a person? His attitude towards Jews cannot be coherently allied with other aspects of his character and personality. We have a rich variety of ways we can express this sort of judgment. We can say that the camp commander is evil but that is insufficient to explain what is peculiar about the moral wrongness involved. It is better to make a judgment which draws from the contradictory nature of his character and personality: he is *confused*, perhaps *sick,* and the confusion arises from his having accepted too willingly the Nazi culture of which he has become a part, so he is also of a *weak* character. We can say he is better, or capable of better, than this, again drawing from aspects to him that we judge to be good. To make these sorts of judgments we have in some, not all, important respects to step outside what the camp commander is like historically and mentally. Crudely, we make judgments about what he is 'really like' without merely reporting his mental life.

But the camp commander's case is an extraordinary and terrible one. How much more easily can we understand the idea in a person who is not engaged in evil. Consider the following kind of case. A talented and ambitious pianist who suffers badly from stage fright loses the tip of a finger on a lawn mower. Despite the fact that this will only be a temporary setback she promptly gives up the piano and begins another career. She says that the accident was 'the best thing that happened to her' and that she is now 'happy and free' of the terrible stage fright she suffered. I suggest that we would say that, despite her (true) description of how she felt (her incorrigible report of her mental life), her description did not recount properly what she was really committed to in her life. We say: she is making a mistake. *Of course*, it would be wrong to be arrogant about these judgments; we might be wrong. But that is not to alter the point that these judgments can be made and that we regard judgments about a person's commitments as superior to that person's reports of their mental life. Indeed, we might well say of the pianist that 'she is not really happy', or that she is 'fooling herself'.

If there is a sense in which we can say that a person who means, intends and acts in particular ways is not actually committed (or, with considerably more explanatory power, better described as confused, or even ill) to these courses of action, think how much more strongly this idea applies to cases of action and meaning where a *number* of people are involved. If eight people, working together in a group, combine their views in some rule-like way (S is the 'spokesman', for example), how much more easily it would be to say 'despite what S means' his words do not express the group's commitments. This all the more specially so if we understand by 'S' not a particular person but a rule-created office: that S refers to a legislative-type stamp placed upon the particular spokesman who happens to be occupying that office at that particular time. We cannot say just simply that the rules give him absolute authority to speak for the group since we are taken by the sense of commitment expressed in the group's giving S the authority to speak. True, in part what we mean by 'authority' is its pre-emptory force – the fact that reference to the meaning is all that is required by way of a reason for taking the meaning seriously – but that is no different from saying that, in the pianist's case, and to a lesser extent (depending on the degree of 'sickness' we are ascribing) in the camp commander's case, each person's declaration ('I'm happy'; 'Jews are rats') arrests us – has force – because people's statements of their commitments take priority in our judgment about what those commitments are. But taking priority is not the same as being conclusive.

Art

Music falls into the case of commitment very willingly. The performers take the works on and give them a 'life of their own'. There is a way of interpreting music which is consistent with 'following the intentions of the composer' and which is deadly dull. The performer who follows the notes, the timing, each guide to expression (all the crescendos, the pianos, the metronome markings, often painstakingly gathered from the Ur-texts edition) which can be spectacularly unsuccessful. To be a proper interpretation there has to be a joining of spirits (I am reminded by Beethoven's famous statement on his *Missa Solemnis*: 'From the heart – may it go back to the heart'). As good music teachers say: to be able to perform Bach properly you have to try to become Bach himself, meaning that the performer must try to identify with what Bach was committed to in his piece of music. But I do not intend here to bring out any sense at all of having thereby to identify with Bach's *intentions*.

It is this kind of understanding, I think, that allows us to see that 'finishing off' a work of literature or music by someone other than the composer is a perfectly possible and coherent endeavour.[15] Indeed, Schubert's *Unfinished Symphony* has been finished off many times. Further, there are some sort of criteria of criticism both internal to what the composer has done and external in the sense that it requires creative and imaginative energy from the composer doing the finishing off: a putative final movement which ignored all but two or three key tunes, followed only the outlines of the tonal structure, and scored the final movement for drum machine and 40 bagpipes would probably not be composition which followed the interpretive spirit.

But conversely, joining the spirit of the work might lead to an abandonment of what the composer intended. Just to take some examples: it is part of the tradition of music criticism to say that Schumann was wrong to score his piano quintet for chamber music because it is clearly more suited as a piano concerto. Further, there is a good case for the use of a piano for works that could only have been intended for harpsichord, for example, since the clarity and expressive possibilities of the piano are more able to give effect to much Baroque music. (This applies particularly to the Bach harpsichord sonatas.) An example of slavish devotion to intention is one I can give from my own experience. At a performance of the *Messiah,* because there was no harpsichord available, a piano had thumbtacks placed in each of its internal hammers, to produce an approximate 'clunking'. This was perceived to be 'historically' correct, despite the result being absurd. A proper appreciation of what was required would have resulted in a piano being used: Handel was undoubtedly in favour of something that sounded pleasing. (But there are complexities and difficulties: one feature of baroque music was the experimentation and fascination with the particular sounds of each instrument; that is, it is a feature of the period which must be involved with the composers' projects, and so what I have said should not be taken to say that we need never pay attention to what was intended in the appropriate context).

In literature the idea of the spirit of the author does, of course, make great sense. During the dramatization by the BBC of *Martin Chuzzlewit* for which David Lodge wrote an alternative happy ending (consisting of multiple marriages) there was a heated debate between Lodge and James, the director, who had wanted a more stoical ending, involving, I think, a soliloquy by Tom Pinch. The following was said: 'The endings are not true to Dickens's ending'; Lodge's and James's interpretations are 'most faithful to the spirit of Dickens's work'; 'I don't think it's false to Dickens, who is often sentimental'; Lodge is, wrongly, 'using Dickens to his own ends' (meaning, presumably, he is paid by BBC lobbyists for higher audience ratings).

And the arguments take the form of: '*Martin Chuzzlewit* without the section on America is a truncated novel and so the whole production was flawed' (compare 'the Nazi commander's character was flawed'); and 'since the section on America, which shows Martin in a different and more sober light is removed, a sentimental ending is justified' and 'the section on America was wrong in the first place because that is not consistent with Martin's character in the remainder of the novel'. Note, too, reviews of

Measure for Measure at Stratford which seemed to favour the use of modern-day sets because, to quote one review: 'since used without self-indulgence it allows both the argument and the drama of the work to be revealed more clearly'.

But returning to law, if understanding our legislator's judgments involves understanding all his other acts we discover that we do not need to focus our attention on particular legislators. Our account of describing the commitments of our legislator can be abandoned. We should then realize that our focus there only arises because we have been gripped by the mental state model. Instead we come to the idea that particular statutes are to be understood in the light only of what Parliament is committed to as we understand the commitments evidenced in the artistic artefacts (the symphony; the BBC production of *Martin Chuzzlewit,* the novel, and so on). That means looking not only to what was actually said in the context of one provision of the statute but looking at the context of the statute itself and within the context of all other statutes which Parliament is committed to. We start to justify as a whole what it is that Parliament is committed to. (Indeed, as I suggested at the beginning, the word 'context' is not really the appropriate word here since it suggests a particular time and place; we should, rather, be looking instead at the whole institution of the law, since Parliament only gains its meaning from the entire *matrix* that is the legal system.)

Objectivity

Where do these committed type judgments come from? How do we assess their worth? To answer this question I need to distinguish between two types of interpretive judgment, the critical and the positive.

Critical Interpretation

The interpreter's commitment to understanding the law (or literature or whatever) is expressed critically when the interpreter is prepared to stand by his statement of what the law is in the form of giving reasons other than those of the kind: this is what other people accept. It is also, I think, an interpretation from the point of view of someone who is aware of his ability to be critical about other interpretations including his own. Examples of critical interpretation in the law are those of the usual kind. An example from the case of *Smith* is: 'It is beyond belief that Parliament contemplated that an adopted child's right to obtain a birth certificate should be absolute come what may'; others are: 'dyslexic children have a right to damages where they have missed out on special schooling through the negligence of local education authorities' (a contemporary as yet unreported House of Lords case); 'rape is no longer confined to non-married relationships', and so on.

A good example to go further into what I mean by 'critical' interpretation is the vehicles in the park prohibition. To interpret this provision you must at least have the idea that Parliament has a right, by writing statutes, that its words be taken seriously. It follows that our understanding of that right is part of our judgment whether any interpretation of that statute is correct. It is not, too, that we are *substituting* our judgment for that of Parliament. We are, instead, making a judgment that is not only consonant with but contributes to and is creative upon what has been done by Parliament. There is no doubt that lawyers make such critical interpretive judgments and that they are quite different from judgments of historical enquiry. It is also clear that they are judgments, in some sense, of a personal nature. These judgments, if they must 'come from' somewhere, come from within. In fact, it is in the context of thinking that there is 'out there' an actual parliamentary intention which makes people think along the lines of supposing that there has to be an independent place (the locus of the mental event; an authoritative person) 'where the arguments *come from*'. But often they are highly creative judgments, as when a lawyer proposes a novel proposition of law in an academic paper, a courtroom, or in the course of justifying a judgment. The most novel have little, if any, support in the sense that they have only been hinted at, if at all, in previous decisions or statutes. Those that have been accepted have done so because they are consonant with the law, not necessarily in the sense that they fit in most smoothly with everything that has gone before because sometimes they are successful in spite of the fact that they conflict with some major principles (the *High Trees* principle is a good example) but because the principle they instantiate is so fundamental.

Positive Interpretation

Positive interpretation expresses the uncritical acceptance of a view, generally (or specifically within a group) held. It is the attempt at justifying an interpretation by saying: this is simply *what other people accept*. It encourages the 'read off' sense of a statute whereby the statute is seen 'out there' ready-marked and waiting; in this sense, positive interpretation is in the same category of mistake as thinking in terms of the intention theory. There is a danger of being sheeplike here. It cannot be a conclusive reason for adopting a genuinely interpretive position in law solely that other people have adopted or accepted a particular position. It is for this reason that I think that positive interpretation is not real interpretation at all. And I think that given the lack of reasons of fairness as exist in the law which place a particular weight upon what other people say or have acted, this must be true even more strongly in areas of interpretation other than law, such as literature, music and so on. If we think that proper interpretations can only be accounted for in terms of what-other-people-have-said-or-decided we are drawn to the idea that the law must 'come from' somewhere. It also means that the imaginative possibilities of interpretation are stultified; our imagination is restricted only to working out what other people have said.

Examples of positive interpretation are those which tend to sit silently in the background although their presence is strongly felt: 'What Crown-in-Parliament enacts is law'; 'no judge would accept that'.[16] We refer to these sorts of interpretations of law without, at any rate, much criticism and, in most areas of the law, we mention them hardly at all, simply because we accept them uncritically. They are what lawyers will largely accept just because that is what other lawyers accept. So, for example, it would seem odd for a criminal law student in a class in which liability under the Theft Act 1968 is being discussed to challenge the *legal* status of the Theft Act 1968. It is not just that such a challenge is novel, like a novel way of interpreting a case; it seems wrong, and in one sense is wrong because it challenges what is simply accepted by all lawyers, which is that the Theft Act sets the conditions – it is the starting point – for criminal liability for theft.

The idea of positive interpretation is, nevertheless, an important one (apart from the fact that many of the 'critical' school understand – and therefore rightly attack – only this version of interpretation). 'What other people think', or 'what is generally accepted' is frequently an important ingredient of a good interpretive judgment and so positive interpretations create their own force-field. It is particularly important in law since generally accepted ways of interpreting law constitute good practical reasons of fairness (and, I think, deference or respect) and economy for endorsing the generally accepted way. *Fairness* requires that things continue to be decided in the same way as before since reasonable expectations are induced in people and we think it right that such expectations should be satisfied; this particular application of the principle of fairness surfaces as a principle of certainty much loved by English judges, many of whom regard property law as the central type of law. I think that this reason is the fundamental reason underlying the doctrine of precedent. But applying it because it is there is, nevertheless, positive interpretation. *Economy* of thinking, too, urges us to adopt those reasoning processes which someone else has gone through to come up with a particular decision in a similar sort of case; this desire for economy explains why judges will refer to what judges have said in different jurisdictions where there is no question of an issue of fairness arising. (Judges here distinguish between the binding and the merely persuasive nature of such precedents).

But argument needs the accumulation of wisdom as part of its persuasive power. This requirement encourages us to engage with what-is-generally-accepted in proposing an unconventional position. There are two aspects to this point. First, weight of opinion, especially built up over time, carries with it its own seal, since there is a distinct natural conservatism in argument weighting it towards what is accepted by many over a relatively long period of time. Second, and more importantly, accepted positions enter the language of our arguments and thus become part of the requirements of argumentative discourse. 'That Parliament cannot bind its successors' is stock-in-trade in constitutional law. When Marxists debate or postmodernists talk amongst themselves, the term 'liberal' is so removed from the discourse as to be almost a dirty word. When you hear modern liberals debate you realize certain terms have become works of art: 'neutrality', 'autonomy', 'equality of respect', and so on. It is when a large number of people agree in their independently arrived at critical interpretations that we have a general consensus, a plateau of agreement, that amounts to a tradition.

Judges are, too, in a unique position since what they declare to be the law *is* the law in a very important sense: their saying so makes it so. Nevertheless, we should note that they are not for that reason always right. Any House of Lords judgment is immediately followed by a plethora of critical articles saying that they got it wrong; and the whole idea of appeal would make no sense unless judges *could* get it wrong. But there is no clear reason why the existence of authoritative tribunals should make any great difference in the nature of interpretation between law and other fields, with perhaps scientific interpretation excluded. Let us imagine a society where literary and artistic criticism are regarded as more important than parking fines and commercial contracts. Literary and artistic Booker-prize courts settle hotly argued disputes. Is there really no sense which we can give to there being a critically right answer in such cases?[17]

Having said this, you might feel that I have placed what I have called real interpretation on too subjective a footing; we now have a view of interpreters as existing in a 'wilderness of single instances', as Holmes once described the common law, each interpreter offering his own view. This view departs too strongly from the idea, the appealing idea, that interpretation must be *of* something and that to avoid rampant subjectivism it must be 'tied back' to something. I think the view is largely correct but further explanation should soften it.

First, we might first note the way we ourselves often reason: we take for granted some proposition and then debate in the light of our acceptance that the proposition is true, in the way a detective will guess a criminal's identity on the basis of some hypotheses. It does not follow that, in this form of reasoning, that these hypotheses are true. To put this another way, we can, intra-subjectively, hold fire on making critically interpretive remarks about certain kinds of proposition while making such remarks about others. This kind of experience occurs inter-subjectively too. I can debate with another person, or group of people, on the assumption that certain propositions are not up for interpretive discussion. To switch to literature for a moment, I can (try to) discuss the critically interpretive question of whether *The Merchant of Venice* is not a fine play about human relationships since it deals in stereotypes, with others who argue that perception of humanity in that play is heightened by the use of stereotypes (or that there are no stereotypes in that play) on a shared assumption between us that *The Merchant of Venice* is a play rather than an anti-Semitic political tract. Of course, we can take our interpretive-assumption hat off that it is a play, and then start debating what is distinctive about plays and how they are distinct from political tracts. In these sorts of case, by accepting certain interpretive positions as true, we are *not* reneging on our responsibility to see them in a critically interpretive light; we are instead, by economy of effort, holding fire on them.

Similarly, in law, we debate the instances of liability under the Theft Act on the basis that the Theft Act is a fundamental source of law; or in practically all instances of debate about the proper interpretation of statutes we make the assumption that the clear expressions of statute accurately state the law. But we should be aware that these fundamental assumptions are just like the ones to which I have referred in literary criticism and they should not blind us to alternative imaginative possibilities which rest on a critical interpretation.

To take the striking example first. The student who says to his criminal law tutor, waving the Law of Property Act 1925 at him, 'This is the real Theft Act', is making a remark that makes a certain amount of sense because we recognize it to be a critically interpretive judgment. That is not to say it is a good judgment or even one that is bad but tenable; but it is not a contradictory remark, in the same way as the comment '*Hamlet* is a rollicking good ghost story' represents a rollicking bad judgment but not one that is wrong because it contradicts what most people think. We can attack unorthodox views by finding out how coherent the view is; certainly parroting the views of the Student Union Proudhon Society would be insufficient; we could ask whether the student considered that he owned anything; to test logical consistency, perhaps we could also test that by asking whether he studied land law; we might consider with some scepticism an answer that he was growing up 'within the system' to subvert it.

Nevertheless, it would be wrong to say to the student just that the Law of Property Act is not generally accepted to be about theft. It would be a sensible criminal law tutor who would say, though, 'We are not going to discuss this sort of matter here' and he might, displaying some imagination, go on to say something like 'You have to learn orthodox criminal law before you can learn to break the rules'. I think also that Arthur Scargill's remarks in the mid-eighties that 'Tory law is not law' fall into the same sort of category; we acknowledge that the remarks do have a critically interpretive meaning and cannot be answered by a bland pronouncement that 'no one accepts that proposition'.

I shall conclude with some terse remarks about objectivity. I think that what I say denies objectivity in determining what commitments are apparent in law and art in the following sense: that it does not follow that what people in general, or in interpretive communities, think is the correct way of thinking, is the correct way of thinking. But that is not to say much. On the other hand, saying what I have said does not commit us to the view that we cannot argue about the truth of different interpretive propositions; the evidence is that we do, more evidence than most being found in the courts. One irritating problem is that often an implicit recognition of the banality of positivist interpretations leads people to suppose, not that good critical interpretations need to be made, but that traditions of thought cannot be justified in critical terms. Thus you get fairly common relativist statements such as that interpretations only have truth for those who exist within one or other tradition of interpretation, or as Fish puts it, amongst a particular 'community of interpreters'. This relativist stance leads people to suppose that traditions speak only to traditionalists, even if those traditions have perfectly sound critical underpinnings. The approach, resting entirely on a logical misunderstanding about truth and a failure to understand the distinction between critical and positivist interpretation, lends itself to a political agenda – a retaliation to a feeling of being alienated from a tradition.[18]

Notes

* A version of this chapter was delivered as the introductory paper to the UCL Graduate School's inter-disciplinary series of seminars on the general theme of interpretation, in November 1994. I should like to thank Jeffrey Jowell and Dan Jacobsen, who chaired this (ongoing) series, for their helpful comments, along with Rosemary Ashton, John North, Martin Swales, Michael Freeman and Andrew Lewis. Another version was delivered to the Centre for Law and Society at the University of Edinburgh in May 1995 and for useful comments I should thank Zenon Bankowski, Emilios Christodoulidis and Beverley Brown.

1 I realise that in all probability what the truth of *the thing interpreted* itself might have been the result of an interpretation: see R. Dworkin *Law's Empire* (1986, Fontana), ch. 2.

2 'Meaning' (1957) *Philosophical Review* 377. I admit to a bias in favour of music being a language of sorts in this sense (see Deryck Cooke's influential work *The Language of Music*, 1959, OUP. A few propositions apart, this is a book which I find convincing.)

3   See Saville, 'The Place of Intention in the Concept of Art' in Osborne (ed.), *Aesthetics* (1972, OUP) 158.

4   [1994] 4 All ER 411.

5   [1993] 1 All ER 42.

6   However, it doesn't seem to me that the rules about the degree to which courts may peek around the edges of a statute to see what Parliament was committed to (by way of looking at special committee reports or at *Hansard*) bears very much on this point. The restrictions should be: a) that the views expressed are by members who hold some sort of status to speak on behalf or as part of legislators, and b) the relatively simple one arising from concerns about economy of time and expense.

7   There are exceptions as, for instance, in the well-known *Rylands v Fletcher* rule in tort. A famous paragraph in this case has been treated interpretively as though it were as fixed as a statutory provision.

8   Hart makes this same point in a different context to great effect in both *The Concept of Law* (1994) 2nd edn. Chs. 2–4 and in his *Essays in Jurisprudence and Philosophy* (1982) ch. 2 (his inaugural lecture).

9   [1991] 2 WLR 782.

10   See my *Ronald Dworkin* (Edinburgh University Press, 1992) ch. 5.

11   *The Concept of Law*, 2nd ed. (Clarendon Press, 1994) 128.

12   See Dworkin *Law's Empire,* 331 and Quine, *Word and Object* (1960, Cambridge, Mass.), 140–56.

13   A word edgeways here: I am not sure whether the conception of commitment which I have outlined is quite like Dworkin's idea of 'making the best sense' of, particularly since, as far as law is concerned, 'best sense' means for him 'best moral sense'. I think it would be highly problematic to look for the morally good sense in all other areas of interpretation. There are, however, clear analogies to be drawn between my example of the commitments of the camp commander and the interpretation of what a 'wicked legal system' is committed to. In both cases, we may employ Fullerian type talk of legal systems existing to a lesser degree because they lack 'internal logic'. Indeed, Fuller characterizes evil as a quality lacking in 'inner logic'. (See his 'Positivism and Fidelity to Law: A Reply to Professor Hart' 1958 *Harvard LR* Vol. 71, 630 at 636). Let us, then, try the transference test on the camp commander:

> The Nazi is committed to removing citizenship from a racial minority; unbe-knownst to him his wife is from a racial minority; therefore he is committed to her losing her citizenship.

Dworkin's view would be, I think, that there is an incoherency in the idea of being committed to (as opposed to intending to) removing citizenship on the basis of an irrelevant characteristic such as race. In the ideal world we pummel the Nazi with argument, pointing out his lack of rationality, until he comes to see it. Acknowledging that our moral views (one form of our commitments) should be subject to reasonable constraints of rationality allows us not to take seriously the sincerely held view that homosexuality is wrong because it causes earthquakes – as the Emperor Justinian was supposed to believe? See Hart, *Law, Liberty and Morality* (1963, OUP), 50.

14   But UK constitutional lawyers are, in the main, well out of touch with this idea. Take, for example, Wade's *Administrative Law* 7th edn. (1994) where it is blandly stated, at p. 32, that judges 'can only obey the latest expression of the will of Parliament'. Throughout this influential textbook, the author demonstrates his belief that Parliament is a person (living now) whose power is entirely self-defined by 'intention'. His doubts